Giovanni Arrighi

Verso

The Geometry of Imperialism

The Limits of Hobson's Paradigm

Translated by Patrick Camiller

© NLB 1978
Verso Editions 1983

Verso Editions and NLB
15 Greek Street, London W1

Filmset in Century Schoolbook by
Servis Filmsetting Ltd, Manchester

Printed by
The Thetford Press Ltd
Thetford, Norfolk

SBN 86091 766 5

Contents

Acknowledgments

The central themes of this book represent the precipitate of seven years' reflection on the misunderstandings that haunt theoretical debate on imperialism. During that time, I have periodically compared my views on international economics and politics with those of Brian Van Arkadie and André Gunder Frank, which have often differed from mine. Their contribution to the ideas set out here is certainly greater than they themselves think. Another, but no less profound influence has been Romano Madera, who made me conscious, in daily political practice prior even to theoretical discussions, of the divergences between the rules of political and of scientific work. It was above all Gianni Massironi, Cristina Piva and Daniel Gabay (who suggested the idea of diagrammatic representation to me) who finally persuaded me to bring my long efforts to develop an unambiguous critique of the theory of imperialism to a conclusion. If I have succeeded in improving that critique, I owe it to those who have had the patience to read and comment on the original version of the manuscript, and in particular to Samir Amin, Perry Anderson, Francesco Fenghi, Laura Fiocco, Alberto Martinelli and Salvatore Veca. If I have not succeeded, the responsibility lies exclusively with me and with those few – Giorgio, Sisa and Ombretta – whose ironic insistence has compelled me to close this work.

Cosenza, September 1977   Giovanni Arrighi

What we have to mention in order to explain the significance, I mean the importance, of a concept, are often extremely general facts of nature: such facts as are hardly ever mentioned because of their great generality.

Ludwig Wittgenstein

Introduction

The purpose of this essay is to contribute towards a resolution of the confusion, as much or more terminological as conceptual, on which the renewal of theoretical debate on imperialism has tended to run aground. Until some concrete steps are taken in this direction, real communication between exponents of diverse theories will continue to be precluded: debate will, at the very most, clarify for each participant *his own* point of view, but it will be unable to establish communication between *different* points of view.

This problem was demonstrated at the seminar organized in Oxford in 1969–70, the aim of which was to 'start a discussion on the theoretical aspects of imperialism between Marxists and non-Marxists, and among Marxists with rather varied approaches'.[1] According to one of the two organizers, the seminar

---

[1] Bob Sutcliffe, 'Conclusion' to *Studies in the Theory of Imperialism*, London 1972, p. 313. The importance of this seminar as a turning-point in the theoretical debate on imperialism has been underlined by Michael Barratt Brown: 'Ten years ago an attempt by this writer to call together a seminar of economists and historians, to consider the problems of imperialism led to a meeting of just four people. A renewed attempt at Oxford in 1969 produced several gatherings of over a hundred social scientists and more than a score of papers, several of them subsequently collected together in one volume.' (*The Economics of Imperialism*, London 1974, p. 17.) At one of these gatherings, I presented a paper in which I argued that, after the Second World War, imperialism assumed characteristics radically different from those that Hobson and Lenin had attributed to it. During the discussion, someone asked me whether I did not think that, by dint of filling 'old bottles' (the theory of imperialism) with 'new wine' (the novel content being lent to the theory), we would end up no longer knowing what was being discussed. I very rapidly perceived the significance of this remark, and thus began the process of reflection that led to this essay.

'succeeded to the extent that many of the participants felt clearer about their own views at the end than they had been at the beginning. But in other ways it failed; on many occasions discussions of some vehemence were conducted at what were obviously cross purposes'.[2]

Both Sutcliffe and Owen put this lack of communication down to the 'profound ambiguity' of the term imperialism. In particular, Sutcliffe observes that:

> Marxists since Lenin have in fact fluctuated in their use of the term imperialism. Very often it is used to describe the whole capitalist system; just as often it refers to the relations between advanced and backward countries within the system. Sometimes it is used in both senses simultaneously, either with, or more often without, an acknowledgement of the ambiguity involved. On the whole when Marxist writers in the last two or three decades have written about the theory of imperialism, they have been writing about underdevelopment and the international aspects of capitalism. This ambiguity, therefore, lies at the roots of misunderstandings among Marxists and between Marxists and non-Marxists; and it leads to the failure to effect a marriage between Lenin's writing on imperialism and contemporary Marxist writing about underdevelopment. It is, therefore, much more than a semantic question.[3]

Accepting these premises, I resolved to attempt a *reconstruction* of the theory of imperialism. This would, I hoped, make it possible to dissipate some of the major ambiguities currently surrounding the theory, and thus to provide new foundations for the resumption of debate on it.

The first difficulty I encountered was to know what exact significance to attach to Lenin's famous definition of imperialism as 'the monopoly stage of capitalism' – a stage which is at the same time characterized as 'the last' or 'the highest'. This formulation may in fact be interpreted in two quite distinct ways: as a *statement of fact* and as a *postulate of identity*.

In the former case, 'imperialism' and 'monopoly stage of capitalism' refer to different ensembles of phenomena which the definition brings into *inter-relationship* without identifying the one with the other. The precise character of these ensembles and of the relation which unites them have then to be determined by reference to other, as yet implicit, definitions, which must be inferred from the context in which the statement was formulated. But, at any event, this reading implies that the definition is submitted to some kind of empirical verification. If it is instead regarded as a postulate of identity, then 'imperialism' or 'monopoly stage of capitalism' designate the *same* ensemble of phenomena, and the definition escapes all empirical control. We may well ask what is the utility of designating the same object – that is, the same ensemble of phenomena – by different terms; and we shall later attempt an answer. But it would make no sense to ask whether the proposition is true or false.

The problem arises because Lenin's writings permit either reading of the definition. Since it is generally interpreted as a postulate of identity, we shall seek first of all to demonstrate that Lenin's arguments can on the contrary warrant us to read it as a statement of fact.

Shortly before formulating his famous definition, Lenin observed that: 'Colonial policy and imperialism existed before the latest stage of capitalism, and even before capitalism. Rome, founded on slavery, pursued a colonial policy and practised imperialism. But "general" disquisitions on imperialism, which ignore, or put in the background, the fundamental difference between socio-economic formations, inevitably turn into the most vapid banality and bragging, like the comparison: "Greater Rome and Greater Britain". Even the capitalist colonial policy of *previous* stages of capitalism is essentially different from the colonial policy of finance capital.'[4] It would appear, then, that for Lenin, imperialism is not *the same thing* as capitalism or one of its stages – even though, in order to

---

[4] V. I. Lenin, 'Imperialism: The Highest Stage of Capitalism', in *Selected Works*, Vol. 1, Moscow 1970, p. 731. Emphasis in the original.

avoid 'banalities' which distract attention from the concrete forms assumed by the phenomenon in different epochs, he defines imperialism *by its relation* to the 'socio-economic formation' with which it co-exists at a given historical moment.

In other words, definition of imperialism must be *historically determinate*: its validity must be continually checked against the events and tendencies observable at a particular moment or in a given situation. It is not by chance that, just when he was formulating his definition, Lenin felt the need to warn that *no* definition 'can [ever] embrace all the concatenations of a phenomenon in its full development' or possess more than 'a conditional and relative value'.[5]

But if imperialism was not, for Lenin, the same thing as the monopoly stage of capitalism, although it had to be defined in relation to it, what then did he designate by the term? The answer does not lie in an explicit definition. For, as we have just seen, what is the object of our enquiry was probably regarded by Lenin as too obvious and banal to require explicit treatment. The solution should rather be sought in the *meaning*, that is the purpose, of the text in which his initial formulation was to be found.

From this point of view, it is enough simply to leaf through *Imperialism: The Highest Stage of Capitalism* in order to realize that Lenin's aim was to demolish Kautsky's theses on 'ultra-imperialism', or the theoretical and practical possibility of a return to a relatively peaceful capitalism. This polemic provides the context in which we should seek the significance attached by Lenin not only to the term 'imperialism', but also to the principle that definitions ought to be historically determinate. In fact, Lenin attacked the very manner in which Kautsky posed the problem:

> 'From the purely economic point of view,' writes Kautsky, 'it is not impossible that capitalism will yet go through a new phase, that of the extension of the policy of the cartels to foreign policy, the phase of ultra-imperialism', i.e., of a super-imperialism, of a union of the imperialisms of the whole world and not struggles among them, a phase of 'the joint exploitation of the world by internationally

5 Ibid., p. 737.

united finance capital'. . . .

If the purely economic point of view is meant to be a 'pure' abstraction, then all that can be said reduces itself to the following proposition: development is proceeding towards monopolies, hence, towards a single world monopoly, towards a single world trust. This is indisputable, but it is also completely meaningless, as is the statement that 'development is proceeding' towards the manufacture of foodstuffs in laboratories. In this sense the 'theory' of ultra-imperialism is no less absurd than a 'theory of ultra-agriculture' would be. If, however, we are discussing the 'purely economic' conditions of the epoch of finance capital as a historically concrete epoch which began at the turn of the twentieth century, then the best reply that one can make to the lifeless abstractions of 'ultra-imperialism' . . . is to contrast them with the concrete economic realities of the present-day world economy.[6]

For Lenin, then, the imperative that definitions be historically determinate was an obligation to anchor his own polemic with Kautsky in the concrete, observable realities of the world economy at a given historical moment. The character of these realities is set out a little later when Lenin, basing himself on the thesis of 'uneven development', perhaps his most original contribution to the theory of imperialism, maintains that *the tendency towards war between imperialist states has become a permanent and definitive feature of the world capitalist system*:

Finance capital and the trusts do not diminish but increase the differences in the rate of growth of the various parts of the world economy. . . . Capitalism is growing with the greatest rapidity in the colonies and in the overseas countries. Among the latter, *new* imperialist powers are emerging (e.g. Japan). The struggle among the world imperialisms is becoming more acute. The tribute levied by finance capital on the most profitable colonial and overseas enterprises is increasing. In the division of this booty, an exceptionally large part goes to countries which do not always stand at the top of the list in the rapidity of the development of their productive forces . . . The question is: what means other than war could there be *under capitalism* to overcome the disparity between the development of productive forces and the accumulation of capital on the one side, and the division of colonies and spheres of influence for finance capital on the other?[7]

[6] Ibid., pp. 740–1.
[7] Ibid., pp. 743–4. Emphasis in the original.

The question is evidently a rhetorical one. But in order to avoid ambiguity, Lenin reiterates with yet greater force in the concluding pages of the pamphlet:

> The only conceivable basis under capitalism for the division of spheres of influence, interests, colonies, etc. is a calculation of the strength of those participating, their general economic, financial, military strength, etc. The strength of these participants in the division does not change to an equal degree, for the *even* development of different undertakings, trusts, branches of industry, or countries is impossible under capitalism . . . Therefore, in the realities of the capitalist system . . . 'inter-imperialist' or 'ultra-imperialist' alliances, no matter what form they may assume, whether of one imperialist coalition against another, or of a general alliance embracing *all* the imperialist powers, are *inevitably* nothing more than a 'truce' in periods between wars.[8]

These citations make it clear that 'at the bottom' of Lenin's discourse on imperialism, *even when he was speaking of monopoly or finance capital*, of the export of capital, parasitism or other aspects, lay *the constancy of the tendency to war between rival capitalist countries* – the tendency which specifically characterized the historical moment in which he was writing. When he employed the term 'imperialism', he was referring to this tendency, which he defined in relation to 'monopoly capital'. The reference must have seemed to him too evident and commonplace to call for explicit treatment. Exploration of it would, moreover, have carried him onto the terrain of 'general disquisitions', where his divergences with Kautsky risked being overshadowed. For us, however, the reference is essential, if we wish to read Lenin's definition of imperialism not as a simple postulate of identity, but as a statement of fact. The definition could then be expressed thus: imperialism, or the tendency to war between capitalist countries, is a necessary consequence of the transformation of capitalism into monopoly or finance capital. Since this transformation is in turn characterized as an irreversible trend – and on this point, at least, there was no difference between Lenin and Kautsky – the

[8] Ibid., p. 761. Emphasis in the original.

corollary follows: monopoly capital as well as its necessary consequence (the tendency to war between rival capitalist countries) represent the final or the highest stage of capitalism.

This vision could not find a better synthesis than in the concluding passage of Lenin's preface to Bukharin's *Imperialism and World Economy*:

> There is no doubt that the development is going *in the direction* of a single world trust that will swallow up all enterprises and all states without exception. But the development in this direction is proceeding under such stress, with such a tempo, with such contradictions, conflicts, and convulsions – not only economical, but also political, national, etc., etc. – that before a single world trust will be reached, before the respective national finance capitals will have formed a world union of 'ultra-imperialism', imperialism will inevitably explode, capitalism will turn into its opposite.[9]

If we now put this vision into a historical perspective, two things must strike us at once: its consistency with the characteristic scenario of the thirty years that followed its formulation; and its growing irrelevance to the situation which has gradually emerged in the thirty years since the Second World War.

An observer of the world politico-economic system of the 30's and the first half of the 40's could not fail to have been impressed by the predictive capacity of Lenin's 'model'. It is true that some of the more attentive witnesses had already noticed the emergence of a number of anomalies, above all those concerning the concept of 'finance capital' (cf. §§22–23).[10] But on the whole, Lenin's estimate of a progressive decline in capitalist market competition, accompanied by accentuated rivalry between capitalist states on the politico-military level, was fully confirmed by the near-complete breakdown of the world market in the 30's and the concomitant tendency to armed conflict between capitalist countries which later issued in the Second World War. Even the Soviet revolution could appear as

[9] V. I. Lenin, 'Introduction' to N. Bukharin, *Imperialism and World Economy*, London 1972, p. 14.
[10] Unless otherwise indicated, section and chapter references apply to the following essay.

a practical confirmation of the validity of this vision, as well as a first partial verification of the judgment that 'imperialism must inevitably explode, and capitalism turn into its opposite'.

However, the events of the next thirty years demonstrate that even the most felicitous definition has a 'relative and conditional value' and can never 'embrace all the concatenations of a phenomenon in its full development' – as Lenin himself had warned in formulating his definition of imperialism. In fact, the unity of the world market was re-established and once again became the typical, though not exclusive, 'site' of capitalist competition. At the same time, rivalry between capitalist countries on the politico-military level has ceased to play a role of any prominence; while instead of a fresh division of the world among the states of these countries, the post-war epoch has witnessed their return to their own national boundaries. Concomitantly with this reversal of the trend that marked the capitalist world during the previous thirty years, the Soviet Union has for many ceased to appear as the embryo of a new world – the 'opposite' into which capitalism should have transformed itself – and become ever more like the centre of a new empire, not in the sense which the term had meanwhile acquired in Marxist theory, but in the traditional acceptation of a 'hierarchical order among states'.

These assertions will be explained and qualified in the course of the essay that follows (particularly in Chapter 3). They are made at this point solely in order to stress the fact that major events and trends since the end of the Second World War constitute *macroscopic anomalies* with regard to Lenin's theory of imperialism; and that the inability of Marxists to grasp them as such is perhaps the principal cause of the ambiguities and misunderstandings on which the theoretical debate of the 60's and 70's has run aground. Faced with the emergence of these anomalies, most Marxists failed to heed Lenin's warning of the relative and conditional value of every definition – all more cogent in the case of a definition that was avowedly historically determinate – and refused to abandon Lenin's characterization of imperialism. The predominant response was instead to preserve the definition by withdrawing it from empirical verification; that is to say, by re-interpreting it as a 'historically indeterminate' postulate of identity.

'Imperialism' and 'monopoly stage of capitalism' have in effect been converted into synonyms. Since Marxists have been unable or unwilling to admit that imperialism, the monopoly stage of capitalism, was not after all the highest stage of capitalism, they have progressively *extended* the meaning of the two synonyms so as to make them comprehend the whole range of phenomena which have characterized capitalism in the post-war period. Consequently, not only have diverse terms (imperialism, monopoly capital, finance capital, etc.) come to designate the same phenomenon, but each and all of these terms have come to designate different, and even anti-thetical, phenomena: war and peace, suppression and reactivation of market competition, portfolio and direct investment, and so on. The very expression 'uneven development', by which Lenin referred to the reversal of the relative positions of advanced and backward countries, has come to assume the opposite significance of a *widening* gulf between such positions.

It is no wonder, then, that by the end of the 60's, what had once been 'the pride' of Marxism – the theory of imperialism[11] – had become a 'Tower of Babel', in which not even Marxists knew any longer how to find their way. The truly surprising thing is that even those scholars who were most alert to the changing pattern of international capitalist relations, felt obliged to pay a tribute to Lenin where none was due, compounding the confusion.[12]

[11] According to Sutcliffe, for example, practically 'all discussions of imperialism at a theoretical level assign importance to the Marxist theory – either as an explanation which is satisfactory or one which is erroneous but requiring challenge . . . Hardly any non-Marxist economist gives serious consideration to the Marxist theory of value, for instance; but very few historians on the question fail to acknowledge what they conceive to be the Marxist theory of imperialism.' Op. cit., p. 312.

[12] I am referring especially to the works of Harry Magdoff (*The Age of Imperialism*, New York and London 1970) and James O'Connor ('The Economic Meaning of Imperialism', in R. I. Rhodes (ed.), *Imperialism and Underdevelopment: A Reader*, New York 1970. While providing an extremely accurate analysis of post-war American imperialism, they seem to argue that Lenin's theses are not only still valid, but are even more so than when they were initially formulated.

Such attachment to Lenin's paradigm[13] was not in itself without a certain justification, even from a strictly scientific point of view. In the natural sciences, too, 'once it has achieved the status of paradigm, a scientific theory is declared invalid only if an alternate candidate is available to take its place. No process yet disclosed by the historical study of scientific development at all resembles the methodological stereotype of falsification by direct comparison with nature. . . . The act of judgment that leads scientists to reject a previously accepted theory is always based upon more than a comparison of that theory with the world. The decision to reject one paradigm is always simultaneously the decision to accept another, and the judgment leading to that decision involves the comparison of both paradigms with nature *and* with each other.'[14]

From this second point of view, the confrontation did not give much ground for comfort. In practice, abandonment of Lenin's paradigm was generally associated with the thesis of 'the end of imperialism', which stood in evident contrast to the 'imperial' role assumed by the United States on a world scale after the Second World War. Moreover, the criticisms levelled against Lenin's theory were often based on manifest distortions of the spirit and the letter of his writings, and, as a rule, attacked him at his strongest point or his fidelity to the scenario of the first half of the 20th century.[15] Thus, if Marxists are to be reproached, it is not because they failed to abandon Lenin's paradigm as soon as the first anomalies for it arose, but

[13] Thomas Kuhn defines 'paradigms' as 'universally recognized scientific achievements that for a time provide model problems and solutions to a community of practicioners'. (*The Structure of Scientific Revolutions*, Chicago 1962, p. x.) The acquisition of a paradigm, and of the more sophisticated type of scientific research that it allows, is a sign of *maturity* in a scientific discipline. Without it, the latter is marked by continual competition between various schools, differentiated by 'their incommensurable ways of seeing the world and of practising science in it'. (Ibid., p. 4.) Whatever one may say, the social and political sciences are still immature in this sense, and use of the term 'paradigm' with reference to their field of study is inappropriate. If I employ the term when discussing the theories of Lenin and Hobson, it is simply to emphasize their location within a given field of study and a particular school (that of Marxism).

[14] Kuhn, op. cit., p. 77.

[15] The thesis of 'the end of imperialism' is associated in particular with John Strachey (*The End of Empire*, London 1959). Criticism of Lenin's theory as a

because they never developed a sufficiently *precise and articulated* conceptual apparatus to alert them to the appearance of such anomalies. Novelty, in fact, 'ordinarily emerges only for the man who, knowing *with precision* what he should expect, is able to recognize that something has gone wrong. Anomaly appears only against the background provided by the paradigm. The more precise and far-reaching that paradigm is, the more sensitive an indicator it provides of anomaly and hence of an occasion for paradigm change'.[16]

Apart from certain isolated cases,[17] the efforts of Marxists, during the period when Lenin's conception of imperialism corresponded most closely to reality, were directed not so much towards refinement of his conceptual apparatus, as to mechanical and ritualistic repetition of his pronouncements. Lacking a sufficiently precise conceptual structure, they then found themselves unprepared to tackle even such macroscopic anomalies as those which became manifest after the Second World War. Instead of isolating and ordering these, to see to what their effective consequences for the paradigm were, Marxists took the course described above – *displacement of anomalies from the field of analysis into ever increasing ambiguities and imprecisions of language.*

* * *

The argument we have developed so far may have given the impression that our projected reconstruction of the theory of imperialism could be based on a 'return to Lenin' which would

---

representation of the imperialism of his epoch has been advanced principally by J. Gallagher and R. Robinson ('The Imperialism of Free Trade', in *Economic History Review*, Vol. 6, No. 1, 1953) and by D. K. Fieldhouse ('"Imperialism": An Historiographical Revision', *Economic History Review*, Vol. 14, No. 2, 1961); their positions have recently been taken over by a number of Marxists, such as A. Emmanuel ('White Settler Colonialism and the Myth of Investment Imperialism', *New Left Review*, No. 73, May–June 1972).

[16] Kuhn, op. cit., p. 65.

[17] I am referring especially to Maurice Dobb (*Political Economy and Capitalism*, London 1940, ch. 7) and Paul Sweezy (*The Theory of Capitalist Development*, London 1946, pt. 4).

circumvent the ambiguities of the 'Marxists since Lenin'. In reality, as we have already stressed, Lenin's *Imperialism* is itself not free from ambiguity. If we have found sufficient grounds for reading his definition of imperialism as a statement of fact, we may find just as many for taking it as a postulate of identity. The terms 'imperialism', 'monopoly stage of capitalism', 'finance capital' are employed in that text interchangeably, *as if they designated the same ensemble of phenomena.* This linguistic imprecision, itself already symptomatic of the non-scientific limits of the pamphlet, is the more serious in that the empirical and relativist position of its author continually tends to pass into a dogmatic and rigidly deterministic standpoint. The very passages quoted above, by excluding the possibility of future developments other than those envisaged by Lenin, indicate a degree of assurance which is in marked contradiction both with his warning of the relative and conditional value of all definitions, and with his prescription to keep to historically determinate definitions.

In effect, the terminological ambiguity is integral to Lenin's paradigm and, I think, stems from a confusion of the rules of scientific work with those of political activity. Some Marxists, of course, will reject the very idea of a distinction between political and scientific labour, contending that only revolutionary practice can produce political science and only politics based on a scientific analysis of reality can be revolutionary. But leaving aside the fact that, in the present crisis of the paradigm, it is difficult if not impossible for these same Marxists to agree upon the meaning of this proposition, any militant who has reflected upon his own political practice must accept that, in political activity, 'theory' does not serve solely as a guide to action. Indeed, this can sometimes be a secondary role, in cases where it performs a number of other functions which are in varying degrees incompatible with the most elementary rules of scientific work.

In such instances, theory functions above all to *reassure* adherents of the success of their political action. Consequently, any relativistic and conditional approach, if it is accepted for the purposes of defining the present in relation to the past, is put to one side when it becomes a question of defining the future in relation to the present. That is ultimately what Lenin's own procedure is in *Imperialism: The Highest Stage of Capitalism*. He first asserts that the definition of imperialism must be historically determinate if it is not to fall into the 'Greater Rome and Greater Britain' type of banality; then he effectively maintains that his own characterization, while determinate with regard to a particular historical conjuncture, will remain valid until the final goal is reached – that of making imperialism 'explode' and transforming capitalism into its 'opposite'.

Typically, this function of theory is often closely connected to another – reproduction and expansion of the consensus with which a given party or political group pursues its objectives. From this point of view, the ambiguity of the terms in which theory is expressed, and of the concepts which comprise it, is not a disadvantage but an advantage. A theory which is too precise and too clearly articulated does not normally exhibit great mobilizing power: its distinctive features foster sectarianism and lead to the paralysis of action. Terminological and conceptual ambiguities leave room for forms of political mediation – for example, mobilization of social groups with diverse ideological representations around a single objective; or use of a given ideological representation as a lever for mobilizing a particular social group around objectives which it does not immediately grasp as its own. Thus, the real meaning of the postulate of an identity between 'imperialism' and 'monopoly stage of capitalism' may be an attempt to unify three diverse ideological representations: that of the oppressed nations of the world (to whom the expression 'imperialism' relates); that of the working class (to whom the expression 'capitalism' relates); and that of the peasant or artisanal petty bourgeoisie (to whom the expression 'monopoly' and/or 'finance' relates).

Even more important, perhaps, is a potential third function. Once adopted by a political organization, a theory will often tend to form part of its general ideological representations, on the basis of which its members distinguish, in daily political work, their own positions from the sometimes similar ones of rival organizations. In these cases, theory becomes a kind of *charter* or statute defining the positions of various political groups and parties, and the distances or boundaries which delimit them from one another. Since ideological representations change only slowly and with difficulty, mutations at the level of 'theory' may have far from minor organizational repercussions, especially on those organizations which, like Marxist parties, attach great weight to theory. However, what enters into these ideological representations is not so much the 'signified' as the 'signifiers' in which the 'theory' is expressed. The appearance of anomalies will then as a rule inspire changes, not in the terms or signifiers of the theory, but rather in the signified.

These observations point towards what might be called an anthropology of politics,[18] which is beyond the scope of the present investigation. If they are introduced here, it is solely in order to demonstrate that what appears senseless from the point of view of scientific work – for instance, the tendency to transfer anomalies from the plane of analysis to that of language – may not necessarily be so from the perspective of a more or less conscious political logic. The incapacity of Marxists to specify and articulate the Leninist theory of imperialism to alert them to the emergence of anomalies, may therefore be ascribed not to accidental factors, including possible 'subjective' deficiencies, but to one of the fundamental characteristics of Lenin's paradigm itself – namely, a subordination of scientific exigencies to those of political activity.

Dissolution of the ambiguities of the term 'imperialism' presupposes a reversal of this relationship, so that the anomalies are returned from the plane of language to that of analysis. From this point of view, a 'return to Lenin' offers no solution: it would lead us to a rediscovery *in nuce* of all the ambiguities that have affected 'Marxists since Lenin'. I have thus en-

[18] The reference to anthropology rests upon the apparent similarities between certain functions that are often assigned to 'theory' and those attributed by anthropologists to the 'myth'. Of course, whatever the functional relationships of theory to politics in a given epoch or conjuncture, these are not immutable. They should on the contrary be put in a historical perspective to trace the changes in them, and the greater or lesser degree of variance between them and the exigencies of scientific work.

deavoured to go 'beyond' Lenin, or to go back to the sources of his scientific thinking on imperialism, leaving for a later date analysis of the transformation of that thought into a political doctrine.[19]

In the present study, Hobson is treated essentially as a 'source' of Lenin's scientific thinking on imperialism. Many will probably dissent from this assessment of the relationship between the two. Sutcliffe, for example, argues that the idea of a theory of imperialism common to 'Hobson and Lenin' is a myth invented by non-Marxist historians and economists: 'As is well-known, Lenin was greatly indebted to Hobson for the evidence he produced of the relations between British imperial policy and capital exports. But Lenin owed scarcely anything to Hobson from a theoretical point of view. . . . To speak of a "Hobson-Lenin theory", therefore, is greatly to exaggerate the theoretical proximity of the two. Lenin explicitly repudiated Hobson's theoretical perspective.'[20]

It seems to me that this standpoint conflicts both with Lenin's explicit acknowledgment, in the preface to his work,[21] of his scientific debt to Hobson and Hilferding, and with Lenin's continual references to the theses or hypotheses of Hobson which he had made his own and placed at the centre of his analysis. I have in mind not only, nor even primarily, the hypothesis of a link between export of capital and territorial expansion (here even Sutcliffe concedes Lenin's debt), nor yet the associated hypothesis of a tendency to parasitism in the imperialist countries. I am referring above all to the fact that

[19] I originally intended to examine both Hobson's work on imperialism and Hilferding's analysis of finance capital – the two scientific sources to which Lenin referred. This examination was in turn to be only the foundation for an investigation of Lenin's 'theory' as a form of reduction of incommensurable scientific theories to a political doctrine. As my research proceeded, however, Hobson's thought proved to be so analytically stimulating that it absorbed all my energies and forced me to leave for another occasion the study of both Hilferding and Lenin.

[20] Sutcliffe, op. cit., p. 315.

[21] Lenin, op. cit. (1970), p. 671.

Lenin himself praised Hobson as the first writer to have formulated a definition of imperialism determinate to the concrete historical conditions of their epoch:

> Kautsky, while claiming that he continues to advocate Marxism, as a matter of fact takes a step backward compared with the *social-liberal* Hobson, who more *correctly* takes into account two 'historically concrete' (Kautsky's definition is a mockery of historical concreteness!) features of modern imperialism: (1) the competition between *several* imperialisms, and (2) the predominance of the financier over the merchant.[22]

Lenin's concurrence with this definition strengthens our claim that the question of war between rival capitalist countries was 'at the basis' of his discourse on imperialism. At the same time, it demonstrates that Lenin shared not just a few isolated hypotheses, but the very mode in which Hobson had outlined his *diagnosis* of imperialism. With regard to this diagnosis, the differences between Lenin and Hobson were essentially twofold and derived entirely from the distinct 'spatio-temporal' positions from which they observed the phenomena of imperialism.

In the first place, Hobson had been writing ten years before the outbreak of the Great War, and his principal concern was precisely to point to those tendencies which seemed to him to be leading towards such an event (cf. Chapter 3). Lenin, on the other hand, was writing after the outbreak of the First World War, and he was mainly preoccupied with demonstrating the precariousness of any peace that would follow it – hence his most original contribution in comparison with Hobson, namely, the thesis that 'uneven development' would rekindle the conflict among capitalist countries for a fresh redivision of the world (cf. Chapter 3). Secondly, Hobson's theory referred especially to late 19th century England. Even though, as Lenin put it, this was the country 'richest in colonies, in finance capital, and in imperialist experience',[23] it was also the nation where concentration of the productive apparatus had fallen

---

[22] Ibid., p. 739. Emphasis in the original.
[23] Ibid., p. 747.

furthest behind the levels attained on the European continent, particularly in Germany, which was at the centre of Hilferding's analysis – that other scientific source of Lenin's work. This explains why, in the latter's account, capitalist concentration plays such a decisive role in furthering the rise of monopoly capital and imperialism, whereas this phenomenon is virtually absent from Hobson's account.

However, this second difference does not, as it may seem at first, redound entirely to Lenin's advantage. His analysis remains undecided between two diverse and incommensurable conceptions of 'finance capital'. The sense in which Hobson's conception was incommensurable with that of Hilferding will be explained in our conclusion, when at least one of the two will be defined. For the moment, it is enough to mention the fact that, for Hobson, the expression 'finance capital' (or analogous terms he employed) designated a *supranational* entity which had almost no links with any productive apparatus; whereas for Hilferding, it referred to an entity of a *national* character whose ties with the productive apparatus tended to be extremely close. Lenin continually oscillated between these two notions, without ever differentiating between them in a clear and explicit manner. Indeed, he leaves the unmistakable impression that he draws no distinction between the two, consciously or unconsciously employing a single term 'finance capital' to designate quite distinct ensembles of phenomena.

If we disregard these two differences, Lenin does not seem to have diverged a great deal, at the diagnostic level, from Hobson's theoretical positions. In fact, what Lenin *explicitly* refuted was not so much Hobson's theoretical construction as the political conclusions which he drew from his diagnosis. It is in the latter respect that Hobson, who is normally counterposed to Kautsky, is finally equated with him: 'This is also the main attitude taken by Hobson in his critique of imperialism. Hobson anticipated Kautsky in protesting against the 'inevitability of imperialism' argument, and in urging the necessity of 'increasing the consuming capacity' of the people (under capitalism!).'[24]

[24] Ibid. p. 754.

Even in this case, it is not Hobson's diagnosis of a tendency to underconsumption (or to overproduction, if the reader prefers) which is rejected by Lenin. As Ferrari Bravo has observed: 'The schema used to explain the relationship between centralization and export of capital is rigidly under-consumptionist and repeats point for point that adopted by Hobson: "the inevitable poverty of the masses" and the necessary relative backwardness of agriculture restrict domestic investment outlets, as the rate of profit declines and the possibility of obtaining super-profits from speculative or non-speculative operations on international markets contracts.'[25] What Lenin denied was the view that the tendency to underconsumption could be reversed in a capitalist regime – a view which, as we shall see (§§22–24), has proved to be correct in the long-run.

Having said this, however, there remains a sense in which it is true that Lenin rejected Hobson's theoretical construction. For if we understand by such a rejection the subordination of the rules of scientific method to those of political action, then this was a stance that Lenin certainly adopted. The opening passage of Hobson's *Imperialism: A Study* – with which I intentionally begin the following essay – shows that, from the standpoint which interests us here, Lenin and Hobson were moving in opposite directions. Lenin used the results of his own and others' scientific research within a political logic which led him to 'expand and distort' the meaning of the terms in which the theory was expressed; whereas Hobson set out to define the concept of imperialism as *univocally* as possible and in direct *counterposition* to the tendency of politicians to expand or distort its meaning.

It should be clear by now that Hobson represents neither the genuine or peculiar *object* of the present investigation (which is evidently not concerned with the history of political or economic thought), nor a simple *pretext* for the introduction of a new theory of imperialism. The reconstruction which I have

[25] L. Ferrari Bravo, 'Vecchie e nuove questioni nella teoria dell'imperialismo', Introduction to idem. (ed.) *Imperialismo e Classe Operaia Multinazionale*, Milan 1975, pp. 11–12. Emphasis in the original.

attempted is in fact intended neither as a simple reproduction of the thought of this or that theoretician – a procedure which would leave us with an aggregation of incommensurable points of view – nor as a new production claiming to start from an object (imperialism) which can only be seized within the scientific or ideological representations that are given of it.

Hobson represents rather the *filter* by means of which I have examined the *presuppositions* of the theory of imperialism in order to explicate, specify and delimit them. The result of this investigation resembles a Weberian construction of ideal types, in which, as is well known, certain elements are isolated from the multiplicity of empirical data so that they may then be co-ordinated in a conceptual framework. This framework differs from reality, with which it is not interchangeable, but empirical data must be referred to it in order to acquire meaning.[26]

Our construction proceeds by stages. In Chapter 1, under the guidance of the analysis developed by Hobson in the first pages of his study, four elements are isolated: colonialism, formal empire, informal empire or internationalism, and imperialism in the strict and specific sense of the term. On the basis of these will stand the whole of the successive construction. These four *primary elements* are themselves ideal types of 'expansionism' or 'imperialism' in the broad sense. Their significations are, however, defined in relation to one another through *a series of distinctions and oppositions* which allow them to be conceived

---

[26] For Weber, an ideal type is 'formed by the one-sided *accentuation* of one or more points of view and by the synthesis of a great many diffuse, discrete, more or less present and occasionally absent *concrete individual* phenomena, which are arranged according to those one-sidedly emphasized viewpoints into a unified *analytical* construct (*Gedankenbild*). In its conceptual purity, this mental construct (*Gedankenbild*) cannot be found anywhere in reality. It is a *utopia*. Historical research faces the task of determining in each individual case, the extent to which this ideal-construct approximates to or diverges from reality.' (*On the Methodology of the Social Sciences*, New York 1949, p. 90.) I have said that the construction expounded in this essay is 'similar', rather than 'identical', to a Weberian ideo-typical construction. There are two main reasons for this: the ambiguity of the term 'utopia' which Weber himself uses to define ideo-typical constructions; and the absence in his ideal types of any 'structural' character in the sense explained in the following pages.

as *co-ordinates of a topological or structural space.*[27] The construction thus comes to resemble not only Weber's ideal-typical constructions, but also those of the French structuralists. It might be situated 'half-way' between the two, and in this sense, may perhaps be called an *ideo-typical structure.*[28]

This structure is completed in Chapters 2 and 3, where the four primary ideal types are *articulated* in four compound ideal types, to which correspond an equal number of historically determinate definitions of imperialism: nationalist, formal, informal, and imperialism *tout court.* The aim of this operation is to demonstrate that every historically determinate definition *presupposes* the determination of a grid (or conceptual framework, or ideo-typical structure), from which the definition is so to speak cut away, while the rest of the structure is put on one side or relegated to the shade. To reconstruct a theory is precisely to bring to light again what disappeared into the shade in a given structure, in such a way as to exhibit the relative or conditional character of that which was given prominence by a particular definition (in this case, Hobson's definition).

The elaboration of the ideo-typical structure presupposed by Hobson's definition proceeds both by reference to the imperialism of the power hegemonic in Hobson's day, namely England (Chapter 2), and by reference to the imperialism of the powers which were emerging at the beginning of the 20th century and which subsequently conquered world hegemony: Germany in the 30's, and the United States after the Second World War (Chapter 3). This dual reference allows us to show

[27] G. Deleuze, 'Par quoi se reconnait le structuralisme?' in F. Chatelet, (ed.) *Histoire de la philosophie*, Vol. 8, *Le XX siecle*, Paris 1973.

[28] Caution is needed here since the structuralists themselves do not seem to agree on what may be considered a 'structuralist construction'. In general, it would appear that the procedure in this essay satisfies both those criteria formulated by Deleuze (op. cit.) and the quite distinct set advanced by Piaget (*Le Structuralisme*, Paris 1968) even though, in the case of some of them, the correspondence is highly obscure and/or partial. For example, the self-regulation to which Piaget attaches so much importance is present in this essay only up to the point where (in Chapter 4) the introduction of a third dimension dissolves the closure and consistency of the two-dimensional structure.

how the four primary types of expansionism, which Hobson isolated in the empirical data of the imperialism of his epoch, define not only a synchronic, but also a diachronic order; how, in other words, the ideo-typical *structure* is at the same time an ideo-typical *genesis*, and how the latter possesses a *cyclical and repetitive* character. Thus, two features become simultaneously apparent: the diachronic and synchronic relativity of that concept of imperialism which Hobson demarcated as the specific object of his study; and the capacity of Hobson's ideo-typical structure to order historico-empirical material which he himself did not, or could not, take into consideration.

Since the ideo-typical structure may assume a genetic form, and since reference will continually be made to historico-empirical material, it is perhaps opportune to recall Weber's admonition that 'ideal-typical developmental *constructs* and *history* are to be sharply distinguished from each other. . . . The maintenance of this distinction in all its rigour often becomes uncommonly difficult in practice due to a certain circumstance. In the interest of the concrete demonstration of an ideal type or of an ideal-typical developmental sequence, one seeks to *make it clear* by the use of concrete illustrative material drawn from empirical-historical reality. The danger of this procedure, which in itself is entirely legitimate, lies in the fact that historical knowledge here appears as a *servant* of theory instead of the opposite role. It is a great temptation for the theorist to regard this relationship either as the normal one, or, far worse, to mix theory with history and indeed to confuse them with each other. This occurs in an extreme way when an ideal construct of a developmental sequence and a conceptual classification of the ideal-types of certain cultural structures . . . are integrated into a *genetic* classification. The series of types which results from the selected conceptual criteria appears then as an historical sequence unrolling with the necessity of a law. The logical classification of analytical concepts on the one hand and the empirical arrangements of the events thus conceptualized in space, time, and causal relationship, on the other, appear to be so bound up together that there is an almost irresistible temptation to do violence to reality in order to prove the real validity of the construct.'[29]

The risks of 'doing violence to reality' are indeed numerous, often even unavoidable, but it is as well to understand what they involve. There is first of all an original and unavoidable act of 'violence', without which social science could not even exist. Thus, the initial choice of any pair of 'opposites' (the primary types) on the basis of which historico-empirical material is ordered and structured, is *imposed* on this material from without by the adoption of position towards it, which expresses what Weber called at once an individual 'sentiment' and 'will', and a given 'view of the world'.[30] There is no innate characteristic in things themselves which allows us to isolate one of their parts: 'A chaos of "existential judgments" about countless individual events would be the only result of a serious attempt to analyse reality "without presuppositions".... Order is brought into this chaos only on the condition that in every case only a *part* of concrete reality is interesting and *significant* to us, because only it is related to the *cultural values* with which we approach reality.'[31]

Thus the initial choice by which the object of study is con- stituted unfailingly 'does violence to reality', by imposing on it a structure which is not 'its own', but which derives from 'our' world-view and our 'concrete' will and sensation. This original violence is evident in the *illustrative use* of historico-empirical material to be found in Chapter 1 of this essay, where reference to empirical data *predominantly* serves to exemplify the sig- nificance of the four primary ideal types which are being isola- ted within the empirical data themselves.

I said 'predominantly', because the scientific use of historico- empirical material is never reducible, even in this initial phase, to the simple function of exemplifying ideal types imposed on reality. After all, 'our' world-view and 'our' concrete will and sensation, which determine the position we take towards reality, are themselves part of reality, and their configuration

[29] Weber, op. cit., pp. 102–3. Emphasis in the original.
[30] Ibid., p. 165.
[31] Ibid., p. 78. Emphasis in the original.

is directly or indirectly influenced by those same events which constitute the historico-empirical material, or at least by *some* of them. A war, a peace, a massacre, a famine, a revolt, a scientific discovery will normally come to form part, albeit chaotically and often unconsciously, of the representations of our imagination, influencing the way in which we look at and see things.

In effect, the adoption of a definite position towards the chaos of empirical data must include a position towards the chaos of our imaginative representations of those data. An ideo-typical construction, in other words, must be able to order, in an *univocal* conceptual framework, those great events which are generally considered in a particular epoch to be relevant to the phenomenon under investigation. Reference to empirical data, then, always has a significance over and above mere illustration of ideo-typical constructions – namely, *verification* of their relevance and univocality. At the same time it should be stressed that the object of verification is not a hypothesis, since '[the ideo-typical concept] is no hypothesis, but it offers guidance to the construction of hypotheses. It is not a *description* of reality but it aims *to give unambiguous means of expression to such a description.*'[32] What calls for verification is whether and to what extent a given ideo-typical structure can generate a univocal order of relevant hypotheses.

The main difficulty which I had to resolve in Chapters 2 and 3 was then precisely the following: how to 'integrate' an univocal representation of what are *generally* considered as the major events of the last 300 years of great-power imperialism, with an ideo-typical structure whose primary elements were *already* defined by Hobson. It is here that the problem of 'not doing violence to reality' arises. For while we try to articulate and specify the ideo-typical structure in such a way as to maximize its conformity with certain privileged factual data, we must not confuse such a structure with 'the real', nor claim that it includes more than it is able or seeks to embrace.

Essential to this task of integration was the production of a topological space – constituted as an order of proximity of

---

[32] Ibid., p. 90. The final emphasis is added.

primary and compound ideal types – capable of a *univocal representation** of Hobson's ideo-typical structure as it was progressively explicated. The fact that the topological space thereby produced thus remains pre-mathematical – in the sense that known theorems do not apply to it – does not diminish its importance. For without reference to a *symbolic order*, there would be a continual risk of relapse into the chaos of empirical data on the one hand, and the disorder of our imaginative and ideological representations on the other. Weber's justification of the reduction of historical individuals and their elements to ideal types is also valid *mutatis mutandis* for the reduction of the ideal type to a pure sign, that is, to a 'position' in a structural space: 'The discursive nature of our knowledge, i.e., the fact that we comprehend reality only through a chain of intellectual modifications, postulates such a conceptual shorthand. Our imagination can often dispense with explicit conceptual formulations as a means of *investigation*. But as regards *exposition*, to the extent that it wishes to be unambiguous, the use of precise formulations in the sphere of cultural analysis is in many cases absolutely necessary.'[33]

*   *   *

In Chapters 2 and 3 of this essay, then, I have sought to demonstrate the relative and conditional character of Hobson's definition of imperialism, while at the same time emphasizing the stability of the ideo-typical structure presupposed by such a definition. In the fourth and final chapter, however, I have tried to show *that this same structure is unstable and transitory*. To this end I have introduced a third co-ordinate – defined by a new pair of antithetical ideal types (finance capital – multinational capital) – which, so to speak, 'divides' and ultimately

---

* *Tr. Note.* The term 'univocal representation', used throughout *The Geometry of Imperialism*, is taken from the epistemology of Galvano Della Volpe, as is 'historically determinate definition'. For an account of the meaning of 'univocal' here, see Galvano Della Volpe, *Critique of Taste*, NLB, London 1978, Chapter Two.

[33] Ibid., p. 94. Emphasis in the original.

'dissolves' the two-dimensional structure within which our reasoning had hitherto proceeded.

I do not need to anticipate here an argument which is expressed in the following essay in a manner that is perhaps already too compressed. But it may be useful to explain why 'capitalism' appears so late on the scene – almost at the end of the performance. After all, Hobson's theory is famous precisely for the connection that it established between 'imperialism' and 'capitalism'; and this link is indeed its peculiar and original feature. As the reader will already have realized, however, the problem lies in the fact that the *re*-construction of a theory is an operation which is in a certain sense *the inverse* of its construction.

To construct a theory is to leave in the shade its presuppositions (in order to illuminate its specific object) or even the definition of that object itself (in order to illuminate the connections, whether causal or less direct, which link its components to one another and to the components of other ensembles). This procedure is justified when either the definition of the object of study or its own presuppositions may be discounted; when it is enough to expound the theory for its interlocutors to know or intuit the subject and the purpose of the discussion. The problem of the re-construction of a theory arises when neither of these two conditions is satisfied – when, as is the case in the present theoretical debate on imperialism, no one is quite sure any more what is being discussed and why it is being discussed. It is then necessary to adopt a procedure that is the inverse of that normally followed in the construction of a theory: we have to bring to light again the presuppositions of the theory and to concentrate on defining its object.

This is the principal reason why two-thirds of the essay which follows *intentionally* leaves on one side the concept of capitalism. It was first of all essential to explicate something that was perfectly obvious and banal for participants in the debate at the beginning of the century, but which contributors to the new debate have lost from sight: that is to say, we had to define in as precise a manner as possible that ensemble of tendencies designated by the term 'imperialism' which was brought into relation with the ensemble designated by the term 'capitalism'. The change of perspective does not diminish the importance of this relation. Indeed, it is only when the dimension of 'capitalism' is introduced that the first links of sufficient causation can be glimpsed – only then does a predominantly static structure begin to acquire dynamic force. It is true, however, that the relation between capitalism and imperialism emerges with altered dimensions, in the sense that it is located within a broader conceptual framework, which the original formulation had left in the shade.

This change of perspective is responsible for some of the omissions and schematic features of the following analysis. Others should be put down to our abstention, motivated above, from attempting to include within a given ideo-typical structure more than it can, or is intended to, cover. Yet others, perhaps the most important, are due to the simple necessity to keep the puzzle within the limits of my ability to solve it. Thus only nation-states that have conquered world hegemony are made the object of representation; the social dimension is not introduced, and, consequently, neither classes nor the class struggle are explicitly treated – an omission that also marks many other theories of imperialism; nor, finally, does the essay go on, as originally planned, to examine other ideo-typical structures, above all that presupposed by Hilferding's theory of finance capital.

In reality, as we shall remark in our conclusion, this work is no more than a first step into a territory that is still completely unexplored. There is naturally no guarantee that it will not open up a 'false track'. If such were the case, then Bacon's maxim[34] could be our motto: 'Truth will sooner come out from error than from confusion.'

---

[34] 'Second Book of Aphorisms', *Bacon: Selections*, New York 1928, p. 415.

1.

The Coordinates

Nationalism and Imperialism: The Premises of Hobson's Definition

It is no easy task to define the concept of imperialism. The same term is customarily used to designate diverse, and in certain respects antithetical, concepts. Indeed, theoretical controversy is often based on nothing more than a failure to grasp what is the object of reference.

J. A. Hobson was well aware of these problems when he made the first attempt to put a study of the phenomenon on a scientific footing:

> Amid the welter of vague political abstractions, to lay one's finger accurately upon any 'ism' so as to pin it down and mark it out by definition seems impossible. Where meanings shift, so quickly and so subtly, not only following changes of thought, but often manipulated artificially by political practitioners so as to obscure, expand or distort, it is idle to demand the same rigour as is expected in the exact sciences. A certain broad consistency in its relations to other kindred terms is the nearest approach to definition which such a term as imperialism admits. Nationalism, internationalism, colonialism, its three closest congeners, are equally elusive, equally shifty, and the changeful overlapping of all four demands the closest vigilance of students of modern politics.[1]

In this essay, I propose to elaborate *freely* the definition of imperialism which Hobson develops from these premises. My purpose is to derive a conceptual order that will assist communication among those who claim to stand on scientific ground in dealing with these questions.

[1] J. A. Hobson, *Imperialism: A Study*, London 1968, p. 3.

1. Writing at the beginning of the 20th century, Hobson uses the term 'imperialism' to refer to a historically determinate event: the transformation of *Nationalism*, which had dominated the international arena for more than a century, into a general tendency of states to expand beyond their national boundaries.

The impact of Nationalism on pre-existent territorial-political entities had in some cases been to increase their cohesion, in others to lead to their disintegration. But its general result was the formation of political units (States) of a relatively well-defined ethnic and cultural composition (Nations).[2] Towards the end of the 19th century, however, these *Nation-States* had exhibited a tendency to 'overflow their natural banks', thereby *giving rise* to those expansionist phenomena which Hobson specified by the term 'Imperialism'.

2. In using this expression, Hobson sought to distinguish the expansionism of his own time from the process, commonly designated by the term *Colonialism*, which had characterized previous epochs. Colonialism, in fact, had denoted the transfer of part of a nation to other territories with a low population density – a territorial expansion, therefore, of its own 'stock', language and institutions.[3]

It mattered little that such expansion had normally involved the physical and cultural extermination of the indigenous populations of the newly occupied territories (as had occurred in the Americas and Australasia).[4] Indeed, the antagonistic

---

[2] Hobson defines the image of nation or nationality by means of a quotation from John Stuart Mill's *Representative Government*: 'A portion of mankind may be said to constitute a nation if they are united among themselves by common sympathies which do not exist between them and others. This feeling of nationality may have been generated by various causes. Sometimes it is the effect of identity of race and descent. Community of language and community of religion greatly contribute to it. Geographical limits are one of the causes. But the strongest of all is identity of political antecedents, the possession of a national history and consequent community of recollections, collective pride and humiliation, pleasure and regret, connected with the same incidents in the past.' *Representative Government*, in *Three Essays*, Oxford 1975, p. 380.

[3] Hobson, op. cit., pp. 6–7.

[4] Ibid., pp. 252–3.

and exclusivist character of the enterprise merely strengthened the image of colonialism as *the effective expansion of a nationality*.

On the other hand, the peculiar historical experience of a new natural-social environment, combined with the great spatial distance from the mother-country, thereafter tended to shape the settlers into distinct nations. Hobson essentially shared the physiocratic image of the colonies as fruits which, once ripe, would drop off the tree that had born them – an image considerably reinforced by the experience of North and South America between the 1770's and the 1820's.

3. At the time when Hobson was writing, the term Colonialism still conveyed this dual image of (antagonistic) expansion of a single nation and filiation of new nationalities. But the expansionist phenomena which had become generalized in the last decades of the 19th century, while continuing to be generically designated as 'colonialist', in reality corresponded to neither of these two images.

For what was above all now occurring was not the territorial expansion of the nation, but the *extension of its political power* to territories, far or near, of peoples 'too foreign to be absorbed and too compact to be permanently crushed'. Thus, within the couplet Nation-State, it was the State and not the Nation that was now expanding.

Of course, exercise of this political power required the transfer abroad as functionaries of a number of citizens of the expansionist Nation-State, while others were attracted to the colonies by the privileges which that power would confer upon them. But the settlers' very position as a small privileged caste altered their original national character and prevented the latter from taking any root in the subject lands:

> The best services which white civilization might be capable of rendering, by examples of normal, healthy, white communities practising the best arts of Western life, are precluded by climatic and other physical conditions in almost every case: the presence of a scattering of white officials, missionaries, traders, mining or plantation overseers, a dominant male caste with little knowledge

of or sympathy for the institutions of the people, is ill-calculated to give to those lower races even such gains as Western civilization might be capable of giving.[5]

Thus, the new expansionist wave generated what Hobson described as a 'spurious' type of colonialism. Its main characteristic was dictatorial political rule, all the more unrestrained the greater the cultural distance between the 'colonial' peoples and the expansionist nation. Yet even this political and dictatorial expansionism, which Hobson designated by the term Imperialism in order to distinguish it from traditional Colonialism, had generated, and continued to generate, phenomena of a nationalist type, while accentuating their exclusivism or xenophobia:

> From this aspect aggressive Imperialism is an artificial stimulation of nationalism in peoples too foreign to be absorbed and too compact to be permanently crushed. We welded Afrikanerdom into just such a dangerous nationalism, and we joined with other nations in creating a resentful nationalism until then unknown in China. The injury to nationalism in both cases consists in converting a cohesive, pacific internal force into an exclusive, hostile force, a perversion of the true power and use of nationality.[6]

4. Once he had introduced the term Imperialism to distinguish contemporary expansionist phenomena from those of previous epochs, Hobson found himself faced with another problem. For his chosen expression called to mind still more remote epochs by means of images which were in some respects not only distinct from, but even antithetical to, those he wished to evoke. In fact, the very idea of *empire* was traditionally associated with a *hierarchical order of states guaranteeing universal peace*, in which the imperial power appeared as one state raised above others. Originating in the so-called *pax Romana*, this image had over the centuries inspired not only political philosophers from Dante to Machiavelli, and from Vico to Kant, but also the policies of the dynastic states of continental Europe.

[5] Ibid., p. 282.
[6] Ibid., p. 11.

However, the ascent of Nationalism had sealed the decline of those imperial States which still overlaid newly-emerging nationalities. Attempts to realize the ideal of Empire were increasingly partial or abortive – indeed served ultimately to reinforce and diffuse existing nationalist currents. In fact, such attempts could in general succeed only when they were themselves grounded in growing national sentiments. But in the long run, imperial states with a weak national base (such as the Habsburg Empire) were debilitated by confrontations with autonomous nationalist forces emerging within their domain; whereas those which possessed a strong national base (such as the Napoleonic Empire) came in the end to propagate or intensify nationalist tendencies, both at home and abroad.

In a certain sense, the Napoleonic experience represented the watershed between the 'internationalist' imperialism of the ancient and medieval world and the nationalist imperialism that was to dominate the world arena a century later. At the end of the eighteenth century, however, a policy calling itself imperialist could still evoke the image of an internationalism, albeit hierarchical, which served to maintain peace among nations.

In his *Study*, Hobson tried to dispel just this image. He showed how, in the historical conditions of a world governed by Nationalism (those before his eyes), projection of the State beyond its national borders, even when inspired by the internationalist idea of Empire, could mean only *anarchy in interstate relations, tending towards universal war*.

According to Hobson, imperialist expansionism provoked reactions politically homogeneous with itself, not only among peoples of a well-defined national identity (cf. §3), but above all among the stronger nation-states, driving them in an exclusivist and chauvinist direction:

> The older nationalism was primarily an inclusive sentiment; its natural relation to the same sentiment in another people was lack of sympathy, not open hostility. . . . While co-existent nationalities are capable of mutual aid involving no direct antagonism of interests, co-existent empires following each its own imperial corner of territorial and industrial aggrandizement are natural

necessary enemies. . . . The scramble for Africa and Asia virtually recast the policy of all European nations, evoked alliances which cross all natural lines of sympathy and historical association, drove every continental nation to consume an ever growing share of its material and resources upon military and naval equipment, drew the great new power of the United States from its isolation into the full tide of competition; and by the multitude, the magnitude, and the suddenness of the issues it had thrown on to the stage of politics, became a constant agent of menace and of perturbation to the peace and progress of mankind.[7]

5. For Hobson, in a world dominated by Nationalism, Internationalism could signify only *an informal order among free and independent nations, assuring their harmony of interests through peaceful interchange of goods and ideas.* Without idealizing the so-called *pax Britannica*, which towards the middle of the 19th century seemed partially to have realized an order of that type, Hobson glimpsed in the policy of Free Trade that internationalist spirit which he could not discover in the 'imperial' politicians of his time:

> The politicians of Free Trade had some foundation for their dream of a quick growth of effective, informal internationalism by peaceful, profitable intercommunication of goods and ideas among nations recognizing a just harmony of interest in free peoples.[8]
>
> Just in proportion as the substitution of true national government for the existing oligarchies or sham democracies becomes possible will the apparent conflicts of national interests disappear, and the fundamental cooperation upon which nineteenth-century Free Trade prematurely relied manifest itself.[9]

We shall employ the term *Informal Empire* to designate this image of internationalism. We thereby intend to emphasize, on the one hand, the 'pacific' quality of the image which it shares with the idea of Empire, and on the other hand, the 'impersonal' and formally egalitarian characteristics which mark it off from the hierarchical inter-state order typical of the latter.

[7] Ibid., pp. 11–12.
[8] Ibid., p. 12.
[9] Ibid., p. 363.

Like Imperialism, the Informal Empire of Free-Trade represented a relationship of international *competition*. At least in
principle, however, two quite distinct types of rivalry were involved. In the case of Imperialism, rivalry affected *political
relations among states* and was expressed in the arms race and
the drive to territorial expansion; whereas in the case of
Informal Empire, it concerned *economic relations among individuals of different nationality* and was expressed in the international division of labour. Thus Imperialism signified *political
conflict* among nations, Informal Empire *economic interdependence* between them.

Peaceful interchange of goods and ideas betokened a type of
development of diverse nationalities antithetical to that of
Colonialism: *instead of territorial aggrandizement and elimination of entire populations*, it led to 'crossing' among them:

> A true test of efficiency of nations [demands] that the conflict of
> nations should take place not by the more primitive forms of fight
> and the ruder weapons in which nations are less differentiated, but
> by the higher forms of fight and the more complex intellectual and
> moral weapons which express the highest degree of national
> differentiation. The higher struggle, conducted through reason, is
> none the less a national struggle for existence, because in it ideas
> and institutions which are worsted die, and not human organisms...
>
> The notion of the world as a cock-pit of nations in which round
> after round shall eliminate feebler fighters and leave in the end one
> nation, the most efficient, to lord it upon the dunghill . . . [pays
> exclusive attention to] the simpler form of struggle, the direct con-
> flict of individuals and species, to the exclusion of the most impor-
> tant part played by 'crossing' as a means of progress throughout
> organic life.
>
> The law of the fertility of 'crosses' as applied to civilization or
> 'social efficiency' alike on the physical and physiological plane
> requires, as a condition of effective operation, internationalism.[10]

The antithesis between Informal Empire (Internationalism,
in Hobson's terminology) and Colonialism becomes yet clearer
if we consider the significance of migration in either case. In

[10] Ibid., pp. 188–90.

Colonialism, as we noted above (§3), emigration is the necessary means of expansion of one national culture *to the exclusion* of an older local culture. In Informal Empire, however, migrations have an *inclusivist* function: they enlarge not the national culture of the emigrants, but rather that of the country in which they settle. European emigration to the Americas provides a good illustration of these two contrasting processes – on the one hand, expansion of Iberian and Anglo-Saxon cultures through extermination or marginalization of indigenous societies, resulting in the formation of new nationalities; on the other hand, enrichment of these new nationalities (especially the North American) by inclusion of individuals and groups originating in the most diverse cultures. In the first form, emigration expressed a relationship of a colonialist type, in the second, one of an 'internationalist' type.

One last point should be made clear. Informal Empire, like Imperialism and unlike Formal Empire and Colonialism, represented for Hobson a stable form of expansion of nationalities, that is one which tended to create a homogeneous environment:

> To ascribe finality to nationalism upon the ground that members of different nations lack 'the common experience necessary to found a common life' is a very arbitrary reading of modern history . . . Direct intercommunication of persons, goods and information is so widely extended and so rapidly advancing that this growth of the 'common experience necessary to found a common life' beyond the area of nationality is surely the most mark-worthy feature of the age . . .
>
> Surely there is a third alternative to the policy of national independence on the one hand, and of the right of conquest by which the more efficient nation absorbs the less efficient on the other, the alternative of experimental and progressive federation, which, proceeding on the line of greatest common experience, grows wider, until an effective political federation is established, comprising the whole of the civilized world.[11]

In other words, peaceful interchange of persons, goods and ideas heightens the homogeneity and interdependence of

[11] Ibid., pp. 168–9.

nations to the point where their existence as separate and exclusive realities can be overcome. Colonialism and Formal Empire are unstable expansionist tendencies, destined in the final analysis to strengthen nationalist phenomena. Nationalism in turn permits of two alternative outcomes: *either* Imperialism, that is, anarchy in inter-state relations which tends in the short term to the oppression of weak nations by strong, and in the long term to universal war; *or* Internationalism (Informal Empire), that is to say, free circulation of men, goods and ideas, which tends to increase the interdependence and homogeneity of nations.

6. We are now in a position to synthesize the series of distinctions and oppositions through which Hobson attempted to define and convey his conception of Imperialism. We shall have to schematize to some degree the wealth of his images, but a certain 'impoverishment' of language will probably assist us to understand more precisely the real object of Hobson's *Study*.

In Fig. 1, Hobson's image of Imperialism is designated by the segment NS—S⁺, *distinct* from the images of Colonialism

Fig. 1

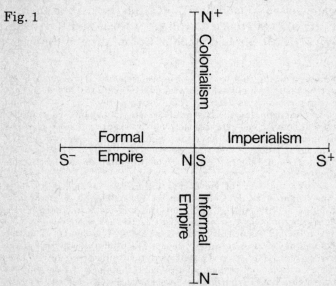

(NS—N$^+$) and Informal Empire (NS—N$^-$), and *counterposed* to the image of Formal Empire (NS—S$^-$). Whereas Imperialism is distinguished from Colonialism and Informal Empire as expansion of the State and not of the Nation (§3), it is counterposed to Formal Empire by virtue of that anarchy of its interstate relations which tends towards universal war (§4).

Colonialism and Informal Empire are themselves distinguished from each other as the exclusive and inclusive (or antagonistic and non-antagonistic) forms of expansion of nationality (§5). Finally, the point where the two axes of State expansion (S$^-$—S—S$^+$) and National expansion (N$^-$—N—N$^+$)[12] coincide, designates the Nation State (NS) as the 'origin' *in an analytical sense* of the four expansionist phenomena taken as a totality.[13]

Nevertheless, we have already seen that Hobson does not confine himself to distinction and opposition of various images of expansionism in order to 'pin down and mark out' the concept of imperialism; he ventures at the same time a judgment on the *stability* of such phenomena in an epoch dominated by Nationalism. He considered that the tendency to form sovereign and independent political units (States), on the basis of entities relatively integrated from an ethnic, cultural and territorial point of view (Nations), had made of Colonialism and Formal

---

[12] The symbols which appear in Fig. 1 have been selected in order to help the reader remember their designation. Thus it should be kept in mind that S and N (whether with a plus or minus) refer to forms of expansion of the State (Formal Empire and Imperialism) and the Nation (Colonialism and Informal Empire) respectively. The signs $^+$ and $^-$ refer respectively to the antagonistic (exclusive) and non-antagonistic (inclusive) character which each of these two types of expansionism may assume. It is thus possible to distinguish Imperialism (NS—S$^+$) from Formal Empire (NS—S$^-$) and Colonialism (NS—N$^+$) from Informal Empire (NS—N$^-$).

[13] From a *historical* point of view, the Nation-State evidently does not represent the origin of either Colonialism or Formal Empire – or even of Informal Empire, if 17th-century Dutch imperialism is to be included in this category. It will become clear as we proceed that the grid which we are constructing has a limited historical validity; and that, in particular, it has no meaning before the Nation-State has become the primary structure of the international system. Its function is purely analytical – that is to say, it defines an object which has no empirical correlates before the second half of the 17th century and which is not fully visible until the end of the 19th century (cf. §18).

Empire 'unstable' forms of expansionism, which inevitably resulted in the diffusion and reinforcement of Nationalism itself (§§2 and 4). For Hobson, Nationalism could spread in only two directions: towards Imperialism and towards Internationalism (Informal Empire) – the only relatively 'stable' forms of expansionism, in that they generated tendencies homogeneous to themselves (§§3 and 5).

We may depict this assessment of the relative stability of the respective forms of expansionism by assigning a direction to the segments represented in Fig. 1. In this manner, we obtain the four directional (or arrowed) segments of Fig. 2, which define not only the meaning attributed by Hobson to the term Imperialism (NS $\rightarrow$ S$^+$), but also a conceptual 'grid' capable of ordering various tendencies observable on the international arena.

Fig. 2

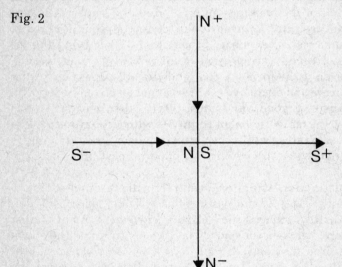

Let us now take this arena towards the end of the 19th century. On a synchronic reading, the arrow N$^+$ $\rightarrow$ NS would designate the nationalist tendencies developing in the 'colonial' world (in the restricted sense which Hobson gave to the term). Such tendencies had been revealed most dramatically during the Boer War, and indeed it was this event which inspired Hobson's *Study*; but they could be discerned in other, apparently quite dissimilar areas, such as those of the 'white' colonies of Australasia and Canada, whose formal subordination to England could be reproduced only at the price of ever more substantive concessions to their independence. The arrow $S^- \to NS$, on the other hand, would designate the nationalist tendencies growing in the centre and the periphery of the old formal empires – such as they still existed. The disintegration of the Habsburg and Ottoman Empires were the clearest instances of this, but a similar process was discernible in Russia, Japan and China, where the imperial organization of the state remained formally intact.

The arrows $NS \to N^-$ and $NS \to S^+$ would, by contrast, designate the fact that Nationalism was going beyond simple dissolution of the 'vestiges' of a colonial and imperial past to transform itself into Internationalism and Imperialism (again, in Hobson's restricted sense of the terms). To a varying degree, both these trends were present in all recently formed Nation-States, even if the former – the tendency to surpass enclosure into separate and exclusive realities and to open out in peaceful interchange of goods and ideas with other nations – was starting to be more typical of countries with a colonial past like the United States, while the latter tendency was starting to predominate in countries with an imperial past, like Germany (cf. §13).

This distinction will prove useful for a diachronic reading of Fig. 2 as a totality of successive phases. Thus, taken together, the four arrows express the 'scissors' movement of nationalist phenomena between the end of the 18th century and the end of the 19th. In a first period, represented by the convergence at NS of $N^+ \to NS$ and $S^- \to NS$, Nationalism restructures the world into Nation-States; in a second phase, depicted by the divergence of $NS \to N^-$ and $NS \to S^+$, the world-wide affirmation of Nationalism poses the alternative: Internationalism (Informal Empire) or Imperialism.

Taken separately, however, the two axes $N^+ \to NS \to N^-$ and $S^- \to NS \to S^+$ designate the distinct trajectories followed by Nationalism in two specific situations – those of the United States and Germany, to be precise. In the USA, after nearly a century of inwardly concentrated effort to forge a single nation out of a multiplicity of colonial societies, Nationalism turned outwards at the end of the 19th century towards the external world, or rather towards an integration of that world within an Informal Empire. In Germany, on the contrary, after a century dominated by the drive to reunify the German 'nation' in a single State at the expense of neighbouring Formal Empires, Nationalism now set out on the road of militarism and territorial expansion, abandoning, among other things, the Prussian tradition of free trade.

We shall explore these designations further in the course of our analysis. For the moment, their interest is merely one of exemplification. However I hope that, in this respect at least, the reader may begin to glimpse the utility of the conceptual grid (represented in Fig. 2) as a means both of organizing in a synchronic-diachronic order the expansionist waves of the 19th century, and of conveying the particular images of imperialism which agitated Hobson's mind.

That the grid has certain limits is self-evident: if it had none, it would not be a grid at all, that is, an instrument capable of retaining (fixing) one set of images, while allowing through (obscuring) another set. It is no less obvious that these limits are intimately connected with the system of values or the 'vision of the world' in which Hobson was steeped. However, as Stretton has pointed out in answer to historiographical criticisms of Hobson:

'Complete' explanation would in principle be coextensive with much of human history in much of its detail; so voluminous as merely to pose the problems of selection all over again. Meanwhile in all common sense there are enough very obvious patterns in reality, and enough values shared by investigators of the most diverse politics, to make sure that a lot of knowledge gathered in different interests will prove useful to everybody. . . . [What we need] is to know more, skilfully; not to know all, neutrally.[14]

[14] H. Stretton, *The Political Sciences*, London 1969, p. 140.

In the course of the next section, we shall attempt to circumvent some of the more striking limitations of the schema so far adopted, making clear its contours and content. But even when all these points have been specified, the grid will remain a grid – one, moreover, that is woven rather loosely. Its utility depends not on the quantity of images which it fixes, but rather on their quality. In other words, it is a function of the goals which Hobson set himself in his study of imperialism and which we set ourselves in our study of Hobson.

2.

The Articulation

Structure and Genesis of English Imperialism

7. The most evident limitation of the conceptual grid set out in
the last chapter and schematized in Fig. 2 is its inability to fix
the concrete image of imperialism of which Hobson *actually*
speaks once he has defined its concept. In fact, he deals only
marginally and far from rigorously with the expansionism of
the newly-emerging powers of his epoch (Germany and the
United States) – a phenomenon which we have designated, in
a passable approximation, by means of the trajectories
$S^- \rightarrow NS \rightarrow S^+$ and $N^+ \rightarrow NS \rightarrow N^-$. Hobson is almost exclusively concerned with English expansionism, to which none of
the tendencies represented in Fig. 2 corresponds unambiguously.

As is well known, despite the protectionist wave that swept
across Europe from the 1880's onwards, England did not formally abandon free-trade policies until after the First World
War. It could thus still appear, at the turn of the century
(according to the terminology we have derived from Hobson)
as a power at once 'imperialist' and 'internationalist'. Moreover, its expansionism was composed of various elements
which gave it a specific aspect in different regions of the world:
colonial in Canada and Australasia, imperial in India, informal
in China, and hybrid in Southern Africa.

It has thus not been difficult for historiographical criticism
to demonstrate, with the support of empirical data, both that
the diverse characteristics which Hobson tried to distinguish
and isolate co-existed in English foreign policy at the end of the
19th century, and that there had been a general continuity in

that policy throughout the century:

> The conventional view of Victorian imperial history leaves us with a series of awkward questions. In the age of 'anti-imperialism' why were all colonies retained? Why were so many more obtained? Why were so many new spheres of influence set up? Or again, in the age of 'imperialism' . . . why was there such reluctance to annex further territories? Why did decentralization, begun under the impetus of anti-imperialism, continue? In the age of *laisser-faire* why was the Indian economy developed by the state?
>
> These paradoxes are too radical to explain as merely exceptions which prove the rule or by concluding that imperial policy was largely irrational and inconsistent, the product of a series of accidents and chances. The contradictions, it may be suspected, arise not from the historical reality but from the historians' approach to it. A hypothesis which fits more the facts might be that of a fundamental continuity in British expansion throughout the nineteenth century.[15]

This picture of the coexistence/continuity of the expansionist features of 19th-century English foreign policy may be designated, in the terms defined in the last chapter, by means of a circle connecting the four segments of Fig. 1. We thus obtain the diagram of Fig. 3, in which the images of expansionism distinguished by Hobson are combined in a unified totality as non-directional components of a single (and generic) phenomenon of imperialism. For Gallagher and Robinson, in fact, imperialism may assume the most diverse characters (colonial, formal, informal, pacifist or militarist) according to the general or particular circumstances encountered by a given power in the assertion of its *hegemony* over the international system.

If the concept of imperialism is identified in this way with the image of hegemony, there undoubtedly appears to be a fundamental continuity in English foreign policy – not only, as Gallagher and Robinson argue, throughout the 19th century, but, as we shall see shortly, during the two hundred and fifty years between the mid-17th century and the beginning of the 19th. In conceding this, we need not renounce the attempt to identify, within the drive for hegemony pursued by a given

[15] Gallagher and Robinson, op. cit., p. 5.

Fig. 3

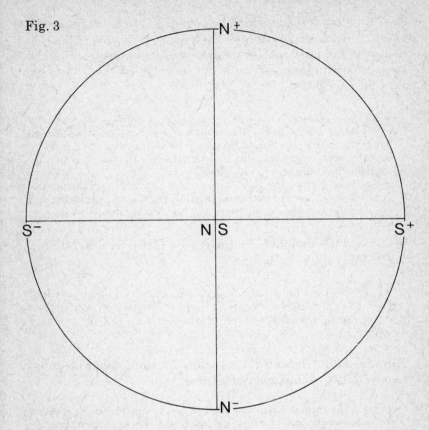

power, either the *overall direction* of alterations or accentuations of its components in different periods, or, above all, the diverse meanings which the same policy may acquire according to the concrete situation.

It is from this latter point of view that we may derive from Hobson certain indications which are ultimately more valid than those of his critics. As a matter of fact, Hobson was not unaware of the coexistence/continuity of diverse expansionist forms in English foreign policy. But he left them in the shade in order to focus light on the elements of discontinuity and specificity in the English imperialism of his epoch.

He stressed in particular two intimately connected tendencies. The first of these, which he considered to be symptomatic of, and supplementary to, the 'New Imperialism', was the tendency of England to elevate the imperial aspect above the strictly colonial one, above all in its relations with the non-European world:

> With the exception of a couple of experiments in India, the tendency everywhere has been towards a closer and more drastic imperial control over the territories that have been annexed, transforming protectorates, company rule, and spheres of influence into definite British States of the Crown colony order.[16]
>
> In a single word, the New Imperialism has increased the area of British despotism, far outbalancing the progress in population and in practical freedom attained by our few democratic colonies.[17]

This despotism undoubtedly remained a factor for peace within the confines of the empire:

> The one real and indisputable success of our rule in India, as indeed generally through our Empire, is in the maintenance of order upon a large scale, the prevention of internecine war, riot, or organised violence.[18]

This should not, however, create any illusions about the long-term stability of the imperial regime:

> Some of the formal virtues of our laws and methods which seem to us most excellent may work out quite otherwise in practice . . . Corrupt as the practice of Eastern tax-gatherers has ever been, tyrannical as has been the power of the usurer, public opinion, expediency, and some personal consideration have always qualified their tyranny; the mechanical rigour of British law is one of the greatest sources of unpopularity of our government in India, and is probably a grave source of actual injury.[19]

In other words, the formalization of English domination of the non-European world did not escape from the general tendency

[16] Hobson, op. cit., p. 26.
[17] Ibid., p. 124.
[18] Ibid., p. 297.
[19] Ibid.

to instability of formal empires in a world dominated by nationalism: what could appear to the metropolitan nation as a virtue of its own imperial domination (i.e., peace and order) could in reality precisely provoke nationalist or proto-nationalist resentment among the subject peoples.

We shall designate this tendency of England as a hegemonic power to elevate the (*political*) formal aspects of its domination above the (*cultural*) colonial ones, by means of a directional arc $N^+ \rightarrow S^-$ linking the arrows $N^+ \rightarrow NS$ and $S^- \rightarrow NS$ (Fig. 4).

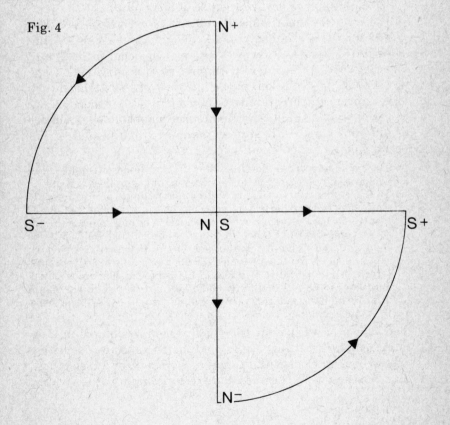

Fig. 4

This representation suggests the unstable, in a certain sense auxiliary and subordinate, character of this first tendency by which Hobson demarcated the English imperialism of his epoch. For in practice this trend was unleashed by the nationalist tendencies mentioned (§6), which were steadily developing in the settler colonies ($N^+ \rightarrow NS$); and in its turn, it tended to detonate others ($S^- \rightarrow NS$) of an imperial matrix. In the last analysis, then, it reinforced and diffused nationalist tendencies, and it is perhaps for this reason that Hobson, while dealing with it as a symptom of the general politicization of international relations, did not place it at the centre of his study.

It seems to me that the specific object of *Imperialism: A Study* is not this first tendency at all, but another – namely, the 'substitution for ambition of a single growing empire the theory and the practice of competing empires'.[20] This competition was not only in itself a token of the 'novelty' of late 19th-century imperialism. By threatening to convert *peace* among the subject peoples of a single empire into *war* among peoples subject to different empires, it shifted the entire significance of imperial policies in the non-European world:

> The expansion of our Empire under the new Imperialism has been compassed by setting the 'lower races' at one another's throats . . . That we do not stand alone in this ignominious policy does not make it better, rather worse, offering terrible prophetic glimpses into a not distant future, when the horrors of our eighteenth century struggle with France in North America and India may be revived upon a gigantic scale, and Africa and Asia may furnish huge cock-pits for the struggles of black and yellow armies representing the imperialist rivalries of Christendom. The present tendencies of Imperialism plainly make in this direction, involving in their recoil a degradation of Western States and a possible *débacle* of Western civilization.[21]

The danger of war among the great powers was becoming ever more real: 'Where thirty years ago there existed one sensitive spot in our relations with France, or Germany, or Russia, there are a dozen now.'[22] The immediate result of great power rivalry,

[20] Ibid., p. 304.
[21] Ibid., p. 138.
[22] Ibid., pp. 126–7.

however, was not war but militarism – a phenomenon which, apart from fuelling antagonisms between peoples, swelled public spending and precipitated the abandonment of free trade. It was utopian to imagine that huge expenditures, determined by the behaviour of rival powers and the new techniques of scientific war, could continue to be financed out of direct taxation. Sooner or later, even England would be forced to follow the states of continental Europe into a policy of indirect taxation, which would more or less openly involve discrimination in favour of domestic industries. Indeed, the abandonment of free trade could be imposed by exigencies of a strategic order, such as the goal of becoming self-sufficient in relation to rival empires, even before it was necessitated by financial considerations.[23]

Beyond certain limits, then, there was *a fundamental incompatibility between free international circulation of goods and ideas and the development of politico-military rivalry among states.* Even if England was still formally a free-trade power, its growing propensity to territorial expansion and politicization of international relations was now – just because of its hegemonic position – decisive for a general shift in competition from the plane of economic relations between individuals of different nationalities to that of political relations between States.

We may designate this tendency by means of the arc $N^- \to S^+$, linking the arrows $NS \to N^-$ and $NS \to S^+$ (Fig. 4). This traces the fact that the policy of the hegemonic power, by fuelling rivalry between states, tended to transform the Informal Empire of free trade into international rivalry leading in the direction of universal war. Whereas Nationalism left undecided the alternative of Imperialism and Internationalism (an indeterminacy represented by the scissors movement of the diagram of Fig. 2) the expansionism of the hegemonic power would decide the alternative in favour of Imperialism (an outcome designated by the 'closing' of the scissors in the diagram of Fig. 4).

[23] Ibid., pp. 100–4.

8. The introduction of the imagery of hegemony, designated by means of the arcs linking the arrows of Fig. 2, has thus made it possible for us to fix unambiguously the concrete image of the imperialism with which Hobson was concerned. The representation given of this image (Fig. 4) has the merit that it shows the coexistence of diverse forms of expansionism within the same policy of hegemony, yet at the same time indicates the direction of that policy – that is to say, the bent of its alteration in a given historical situation. The representation is nevertheless incomplete. In particular, it does not define the trajectory of the continuity discernible in the struggle of the English Nation-State for the conquest and preservation of its world hegemony.

In order to complete the representation – leaving for later a specification of its contours and contents – we shall subject this hegemony to a diachronic analysis. We shall take as a starting-point the passage quoted above (§7), in which Hobson prophesied for a not too distant future a resurgence of the 'horrors' of the 18th-century struggle between France and England in America and India. It was in this period that England conquered the global hegemony which it would retain until the beginning of the 19th century, when Hobson diagnosed its decline. Which tendencies, then, characterized that century, or, to be more precise, the hundred years stretching from the wars against Holland (1652–74) to the defeat of France in the Seven Years' War (1756–63)? How may we designate these tendencies in the terms defined by the conceptual grid schematized in Fig. 2?

First of all, what seems to have been the original and dominant character of this period was a tendency which we may designate by means of the arrow $NS \rightarrow S^+$. The Navigation Acts of 1651 and 1660, by subordinating the colonies to the authority of the English parliament and by bestowing upon the English fleet the monopoly of trade with these colonies, in effect inaugurated a policy of *expansion of the English State beyond its national boundaries* – a policy which precipitated the international system into a period of *world-wide anarchy and war*. During this period, England defeated rival powers one after the other, attaining a position of almost total hegemony over the non-European world. The Navigation Acts directly led England into war with Holland (the prior hegemonic power of the epoch) whose informal empire was effectively reduced to a protectorate of England. The same fate befell the Portuguese colonial empire, even though arms were not necessary in that instance to impose the real relationship of forces between the old power in decline and the new power in ascent. From the positions of relative hegemony which it thereby acquired, England had little difficulty in eliminating the rivalry of Spain and France: participation in the War of the Spanish Succession gave it undisputed control over the seas, while the Seven Years' War brought to an end the secular conflict with France, the other rising power of the epoch, which was definitively swept out of India and North America.

However, the above characterization neglects the 'colonialist' element in English expansionism during this period. Already before the Cromwellian revolution, such expansionism had been distinguished by active encouragement of colonial settlement:

> Although they could not match the Dutch in financial acumen and in the size or efficiency of their merchant fleet, the English believed in founding settlement colonies and not just ports of call en route to the Indies. . . . Besides joint-stock or chartered companies the English developed such expedients for colonization as the proprietory colony analogous to the Portuguese captaincies in Brazil, and Crown colonies nominally under direct royal control. What English colonies in America lacked in natural resources and uniformity they made up for in the number and industriousness of the colonists themselves.[24]

This effective territorial expansion of the English nation beyond its state boundaries could not, however, be fully realized until the Navigation Acts, and the aggressive policy which they initiated, opened up abundant space (political and economic) for British emigration to the New World. England

[24] G. H. Nadel and P. Curtis, 'Introduction' to idem. (eds.) *Imperialism and Colonialism*, New York 1964, pp. 9–10.

was a 'late-comer' in relation to the traditional colonialist nations Spain and Portugal; and only its conquest of world hegemony allowed it to pursue the territorial expansion of its own nationality which was actually accomplished in the hundred years following the wars with Holland. It is also true, however, that without the emigration and dispersal of British settlements in North America, the English state would have found it much harder to gain such a complete victory over rival powers.

The rise of England to the position of hegemonic power may be designated by means of a trajectory within the space jointly defined by the co-ordinates NS—S^+ (imperialism *tout court*) and NS—N^+ (colonialism). If the colonialist component is regarded as a simple consequence of antagonistic state expansion (useful in the consolidation of hegemony once it had been attained rather than in its actual conquest) then it should be designated by means of the arc $S^+ \rightarrow N^+$ traced in Fig. 5. This would then express the fact that 17th and 18th century English imperialism tended to pass into effective territorial expansion of the nationality, the purpose of which was to consolidate a hegemonic position already achieved by the different path NS $\rightarrow S^+$. But it seems to me more correct to consider the two components as inseparably linked, since effective territorial expansion of the nation was *ab initio* an integral part of the expansionist policy of the English state, and since the latter

Fig. 5

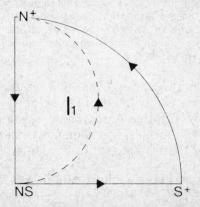

would have had great difficulty in attaining its hegemonic world position without the contribution of the American colonies. If we view matters in this light, the English path to hegemony should be designated by means of an arc $NS \rightarrow N^+$, as is dotted in Fig. 5.[25]

Whichever designation is adopted ($NS \rightarrow S^+ \rightarrow N^+$ or $NS \rightarrow N^+$) it signifies that a hegemonic position (N^+), unattainable through expansionism of a purely colonial kind, has nevertheless been achieved through a combination of the latter with expansionism of a strictly imperialist type, which so to speak institutionalizes a real shift in the relationship of forces between rival powers. This possibility of attaining N^+ does not, therefore, contradict the earlier thesis of the instability of colonialist tendencies (see §6), which is designated in Fig. 5, as in previous diagrams, by the direction of the arrow $N^+ \rightarrow NS$. On the contrary, confirmation of this thesis is essential if we are to complete our definition of the first phase of English imperialism. It allows us, in fact, to comprehend the arc $S^+ \rightarrow N^+$ as signifying not only the tendency of imperialist policy, in the strict sense, to pass into effective territorial expansion of the nationality, but also the tendency of armed conflict between metropolitan states to be transformed into nationalism in the colonies.

This second tendency became manifest only after the Seven Years' War. It represented in a sense a watershed between the first and second phases of English imperialism (§9). Its relationship to the other tendencies analysed so far seems quite evident. The secular struggle with France had driven England to utilize

[25] In this figure and later ones, dotted inscriptions refer to real *historical trajectories*, whether proposed or actually pursued; while unbroken arcs and arrows represent *ideo-typical trajectories*. Thus, in Fig. 5, which as we shall see defines the concept of nationalist imperialism, the ideal type is represented by the ensemble constituted by the arc $S^+ \rightarrow N^+$ and the arrows $NS \rightarrow S^+$ and $N^+ \rightarrow NS$; whereas the historical type (that is, the first phase of English imperialism) is defined by the arc $NS \rightarrow N^+$, which, it should be noted, has a significance only with reference to the ideal type within which it is drawn. On the other hand, Fig. 9 (§12) illustrates the distinction between a historical trajectory that has actually been completed and one that is simply pursued: it will become clear later that the arc $S^+ \rightarrow NS$ represents the former type, and $N^- \rightarrow NS$ the latter type.

the North American colonies as allies on a plane of relative equality, rather than as mere dependencies. This policy bore fruit during the Seven Years' War, when the American colonies showed that they had become an autonomous, and perhaps decisive, force in the definitive defeat of French overseas expansionism. But once this objective had been attained, English attempts to restore a relationship of subordination between colonies and mother-country could not but inflame nationalist sentiments of revolt:

> Anglo-American relations were disrupted because the imperial government clung to its antiquated behaviour and the parting of the ways became inevitable. The emotional driving forces were imperial arrogance on the British side, national sentiment on the American. There was no insurmountable clash of interest, but rather a political quarrel exacerbated by the British government's failure to take American patriotism seriously.[26]

Of course, the conflicts which set the metropolitan powers against one another favoured even more directly the success of nationalist movements of a colonial character. On this point, it is enough to recall the role played by the Franco-American alliance in consolidating American independence of England, and the subsequent role of the Napoleonic cataclysm in Europe in breaking the ties of subordination between the Latin-American colonies and Spain and Portugal.

The birth of nationalism in the colonial world brings to an end the first phase of English imperialism, which we shall term *nationalist imperialism*. Its signification (I_1) is thus defined conjointly by the three tendencies, $NS \rightarrow S^+$, $S^+ \rightarrow N^+$, and $N^+ \rightarrow NS$ (Fig. 5). These trace the antagonistic expansion of the State beyond its national boundaries, in the direction of an effective expansion of the home nationality, but then ultimately tending to unleash nationalism in the colonial world.

9. As is well known, 1776 was the year not only of the American Declaration of Independence, but also of the publication of *The*

---

[26] G. Lichtheim, *Imperialism*, London 1974, p. 54.

Wealth of Nations – a work in which Adam Smith sharply attacked, among other things, the traditional methods of governing the colonies. This coincidence has helped to spread the view that the rebellion of the North-American colonies occurred simultaneously with the onset of a progressive liberalization of English colonial policy. In reality, however, there was no trace of such a change for at least another fifty years:

> That the revolt of the American colonists taught the imperial ruling groups in England a lesson in how to govern colonies wisely is nothing but a legend. Constitutionally and politically, imperial rule was not relaxed but tightened. The rebellious Americans . . . had enjoyed a great deal of freedom in the political respect. Hence, when these colonies revolted while Canada remained loyal, it seemed to the majority of the metropolitan ruling group that this large amount of political freedom had fostered a spirit of democracy and independence which, in turn, had caused the revolution. It was for this reason that the government, determined to keep what was left of the Empire, now embarked upon a reactionary course and imposed upon its old and new colonies a system of centralized supervision and control that was to be maintained for more than half a century.[27]

In other words, the loss of the North American colonies strengthened the tendency of England to formalize its domination of the non-European world and to relegate to a secondary position the informal methods of government typical of colonialism, in the strict sense of the term. Integral to this tendency was the new geo-political orientation adopted by English expansionism at the end of the 18th century: although fresh outlets were found in Australasia after the partial closure of North America, its centre of gravity decisively shifted towards the Indian sub-continent, where there was no room for colonial settlement and imperial methods of government naturally imposed themselves.

We shall designate this tendency of Colonialism to pass into Formal Empire by means of an arc $N^+ \rightarrow S^-$ connecting the arrow $N^+ \rightarrow NS$ to $S^- \rightarrow NS$ (Fig. 6). The division of $S^+ \rightarrow N^+$

[27] K.E. Knorr, *British Colonial Theories: 1570–1850*. Toronto 1944, pp. 112–3,

Fig. 6

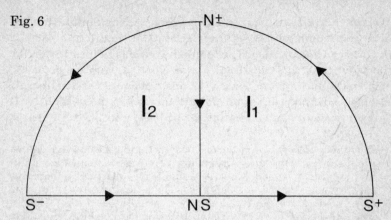

into $N^+ \to S^-$ and $N^+ \to NS$ thus represents that parting of the
ways of England and the North American colonies of which
Lichtheim speaks in the passage just cited. It may be objected
that this designation stresses only one of the two aspects of
English imperialism at the close of the 18th century, namely
the relations which it had come to establish in the non-European
world; and that it does not bring into relief the continuing
anarchy of relations among the great powers. Indeed, much of
the period in question was occupied by the Napoleonic Wars,
which clearly do not conform to the image of peace and order
proper to formal empire.

However, if we examine these wars in a broader perspective
than that of a Eurocentric history, then the discrepancy of
images tends to vanish. It should above all be remembered that
the struggle for *world* hegemony between France and England
had been definitively resolved in favour of the latter by the
Seven Years' War. France's later success alongside the new
United States of America was a purely Pyrrhic victory: when,
following Cornwallis's surrender at Yorktown in 1782, Rodney
defeated the French fleet in the Battle of the Saints, the English
reaffirmed their uncontested supremacy at sea and, consequently, their global hegemony. Nor was that all. the costs of
war had been so excessive for France that it was thrown into a
period of internal crises that issued, six years later, in the
Revolution.

Thus the situation of world-wide anarchy and war had come to an end, together with the struggle among various powers for control of the seas. The Napoleonic Wars had an altogether different significance. They represented an attempt by France to counterpose to the English world empire of the seas, a French territorial empire of the European continent. This project brought it into direct conflict with the old formal empires still dominating the continent, whereas the contest with England tended to assume an indirect, almost 'cold war' character, involving naval blockades and sporadic armed clashes. In other words, the *Pax Britannica* was strengthened at a world level, while war came to be localized, and intensified, in Europe.

Even in Europe, however, there prevailed a tendency to restore, under British hegemony, an imperial organization bringing with it universal peace – a peace that was then effectively realized with the final defeat of Napoleon. Of course, it was quite another question whether the balance of empires laid down by the Peace of Vienna was a stable one; as we know, the restoration ended in an explosion of nationalist tendencies, which, latent throughout this period, led from the 1830's onwards to the progressive disintegration (or transformation in a nationalist direction) of the formal empires of continental Europe.

The emergence of these tendencies, designated by $S^- \rightarrow NS$ in Fig. 6, marked the passage to a new phase of English imperialism. We shall refer to the phase now concluded (designated conjointly by the three movements $N^+ \rightarrow NS$, $N^+ \rightarrow S^-$, and $S^- \rightarrow NS$) as that of *formal imperialism*, thereby laying stress on the formal character which British hegemony tended to assume in reaction to the revolt of the American colonies. Even in this case, however, the principal effect was ultimately not containment of nationalist tendencies, but their reinforcement and diffusion within those very formal empires of continental Europe that England had tactically supported in an attempt to consolidate its own world hegemony.

10. The paths of England and of the dynastic empires of continental Europe very soon began to diverge. The first skir-

mishes in England's drive to convert its world hegemony into
an informal empire appeared in the years immediately following the Peace of Vienna:

> In 1823, the majority of the countries of Latin America were already
> independent. Nevertheless, although republican arms had trium-
> phed decisively on the field of battle, the new nations still had to
> consolidate their independence, obtain formal recognition, and
> achieve cohesiveness. . . . England quickly understood what the
> birth of independent Latin American republics meant for Europe.
> Aware that the old and anachronistic system of colonial relations
> would crumble, it saw an excellent opportunity to profit by estab-
> lishing commercial relations with the newly independent countries.
> Consequently, between 1815 and 1823 England countered the
> colonialist [or imperial, according to the terminology we have
> adopted – G.A.] design of the Holy Alliance by asserting the prin-
> ciple of non-intervention in Latin America. The Prime Minister,
> George Canning, emphasized the importance of trade with the new
> countries in his statement, 'England will be a workshop and Latin
> America its farm'. In order to ensure this business for the English
> fleet – but at the same time fearful lest the United States and France
> launch a policy of territorial expansion in Latin America – Mr.
> Canning proposed an agreement with these two governments that
> would guarantee the peace and tranquillity of the continent.[28]

Of course, it was not yet a question of breaking the recently
established imperial equilibrium, but rather of its clarification
by the hegemonic power. England's purpose was to limit the
operation of the Holy Alliance to the sphere of continental
Europe and to reserve for itself the role of guarantor of the
world order. Nevertheless, the very pursuit of this goal im-
pelled England to draw closer to the two nation-states which
had the most obstructed its imperial designs and to oppose the
dynastic empires on which it had relied in their achievement.

From the 1830's onwards, this turn became more evident.
Methods of informal integration, tested out in Latin America,
were gradually extended to other regions of the non-European
world by means of *bilateral* treaties of friendship and free trade;

[28] A. Aguilar, *Pan-Americanism from Monroe to the Present*, New York 1968,
p. 23.

the widest-ranging were those signed with Persia (1836 and 1857), Turkey (1838 and 1861) and Japan (1858). Where a free-trade agreement was not sufficient to integrate the 'peripheral zone' into the informal empire, England did not shrink from the use of arms – as it did in the Opium Wars of 1840 and 1857. But even then, the outcome was the extension, not of the formal British Empire, but of the informal empire of free trade.

This free-trade image of England was only partially obscured by the colonialist and imperial tendencies which continued to characterize its expansionism during these decades. The colonial expansion which was pursued without interruption in Canada, Australasia and Southern Africa led, between 1840 and 1870, to the occupation or annexation of vast territories – New Zealand, Queensland, British Columbia, Natal, Transvaal, and so on. But however many square miles they covered, these acquisitions were of secondary significance for the extension of English world domination, secured through the policy of free trade. Moreover, this process of territorial expansion was accompanied by liberalization of metropolitan political control over the colonies (it was in this period that Canada was granted so-called responsible government), so that the tendency of formal empire to change into informal empire could be observed within the colonial processes themselves.

By contrast, nothing of this kind was visible in India:

[India was] the only part of the British Empire to which *laissez-faire* never applied. Its most enthusiastic champions in Britain became bureaucratic planners when they went there, and the most committed opponents of political colonization rarely, and then never seriously, suggested the liquidation of British rule. And the 'formal' British Empire expanded in India even when no other part of it did.[29]

It should be clear from the previous discussion, however, that the case of India does not contradict the informal character of English expansionism between the years 1830 and 1870. In fact, the peculiar tendencies of any period 'rest upon' those which

[29] E. J. Hobsbawm, *Industry and Empire*, London 1968, p. 123.

characterized preceding epochs and are, so to speak, conserved within newly-emerging tendencies. As the typical features of nationalist imperialism were preserved within the phase of formal imperialism when circumstances required, so did the typical institutions of formal imperialism continue to be utilized in India, precisely because of its strategic military and economic position in the construction of an informal empire in the rest of the world.

The rule, that is the tendency towards free trade, was on the other hand even more visible in England's relations with the metropolitan countries and its former colony, the United States, than in its links with the non-European world. Decisive in this respect was the *unilateral* repeal of the Corn Laws (1848) and of the Navigation Acts (1849) – measures which placed England at the centre of a tight web of commercial exchanges:

> English ports were opened to the products of the whole world. Apparently, not far short of one third of the exports of the rest of the world found their way into the United Kingdom in the 1850s and 1860s. . . . Little of this came from the empire, less than a quarter in fact. Our largest single trading-partner was the United States, accounting for nearly a quarter of all imports and of all exports. Another quarter was accounted for by the countries of Europe, which were beginning, like the USA, to industrialize themselves with British equipment and ideas.[30]

This structure of commercial intercourse was accompanied by movements of persons and capital which later gave an 'internationalist' quality to the informal British empire. Between 1830 and 1870, emigration from Great Britain was perhaps more intense than it had ever been; its main outlet, however, was no longer the colonies or provinces of the formal empire, but independent countries, and first of all the United States of America. It thus involved not antagonistic expansion of the English nation, but a general growth of nations through what Hobson called 'crossing' of nationalities (§5).

Analogous processes were observable in capital movements, which grew markedly more intense between 1855 and 1870 and

[30] M. Barratt Brown, *After Imperialism*, London 1963, p. 63.

were oriented predominantly towards the industrializing countries of America and continental Europe. The international
system thus tended to move towards something very close to
Hobson's image of internationalism: 'An all-embracing world
system of virtually unrestricted flows of capital, labour and
goods never actually existed, but between 1860 and 1875 something not too far removed from it came into being.'[31]

The *Pax Britannica* was thereby transformed into an informal empire of free trade, which allowed England to extend its
hegemony to peoples and nations which had escaped, or never
been subject to, its formal empire. Towards the middle of the
19th century, in fact, free trade doctrines became the dominant
ideology not only of the young Latin American republics, but
also of the principal nuclei of European nation-states, such as
Prussia and Piedmont. With the Anglo-French commercial
treaty of 1860, France itself entered the orbit of free trade,
which became in those years the general rule in relations
between nations.

The USA was only a partial exception to the rule. Even there,
free-trade ideology had dominated the first stage of the struggle
against the restrictions on freedom of commerce and enterprise
which the mother-country claimed the right to impose on the
colonies. But in 1816 the Northern states began to introduce
customs tariffs to protect their developing industry; and
despite the fact that between 1832 and 1875 the general free-
trade tendency involved a reduction of such tariffs, they were
abruptly raised again on the occasion of the Civil War (1860–
65).

On the whole, even during the golden years of free trade, the
United States remained a protectionist nation. Still, as we have
said, it also became during this period the main pole of attrac-
tion for English commodities, labour and capital. American
protectionism was thus a stimulus, rather than an obstacle, to
the growth of international trade, demonstrating that within
certain limits protectionism and free trade, like nationalism
and internationalism, were not necessarily in contradiction

[31] Hobsbawm, op. cit., p. 115.

Fig. 7

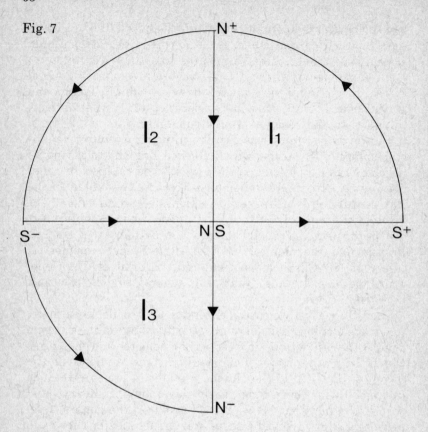

with each other.[32]

In conclusion, we can say that, towards the middle of the 19th century, all forms of nationalism, including the nationalist protectionism of the USA, tended to merge with the hegemonic power's policy of peaceful interchange of goods and ideas, as the regulating principle and practice of international relations. This tendency is represented in Fig. 7 by the convergence at N^- of the arrow $NS \to N^-$ and the arc $S^- \to N^-$. Taken as a whole, the three tendencies $S^- \to NS$, $S^- \to N^-$ and $NS \to N^-$ thus

---

[32] John Stuart Mill was well aware of this fact. As is well known, he viewed in a positive light the protection of developing or 'infant' industries.

define a third phase (I_3) of English imperialism, which we shall term *informal imperialism* in order to stress the mediating role of impersonal market forces in the consolidation and expanded reproduction of England's world hegemony.

11. Whatever 'internationalist' content there may have been in England's mid-century informal empire began to dissolve in the 1870's. As we have seen (§7), it was this process which constituted the specific object of Hobson's study. It may be synthetically designated by the arc $N^- \rightarrow S^+$, joining $NS \rightarrow N^-$ to $NS \rightarrow S^+$ (Figs. 3 and 8). On this point there is little to add to what we have said in the first section of this chapter: we should

Fig. 8

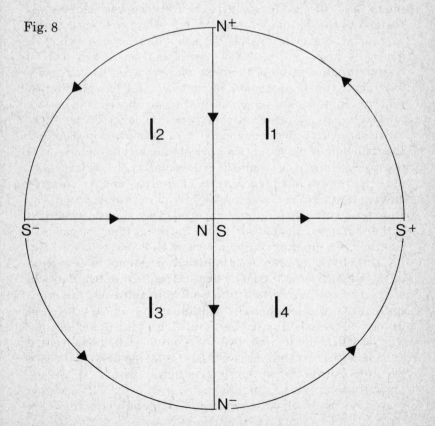

simply make a diachronic specification of the characterization we drew from Hobson. In particular, we need to show the connection between the tendency to full realization of an informal free-trade empire (designated by the convergence at N^- of $S^- \rightarrow N^-$ and $NS \rightarrow N^-$) and the tendency of the English informal empire to pass into 'new' imperialism or imperialism *tout court*.

Of those tendencies which Hobson enumerated in his characterization of the change, the first to manifest itself was the strengthening of political and economic ties between mother-country and colonies in the strict sense – the so-called settler dominions. This objective dominated 'imperialist' thinking in the 1870's, although little of substance was achieved. At the end of the decade, however, there began that spectacular territorial expansion of the English formal empire which is generally held to open a new epoch and which was to be a characteristic feature of the next twenty years. As the reader will recall, this tendency is designated, in the extended representation of the 'new' imperialism (Fig. 4), by means of the arc $N^+ \rightarrow S^-$; we may interpret this as the tendency of the ghost of a past epoch to be 'resurrected'. We have already seen that the tendency in question was the dominant characteristic of the second phase of English expansionism, in which international relations, after a century of anarchy and war, started moving towards the creation of a formal-hierarchic peace. The resumption of English formal-imperial expansionism at the end of the 19th century could still evoke the image of such a pacification, and the imperialist propaganda of Hobson's time relied on just this possibility. But even though the tendency to expansion of the English formal empire had in itself exhibited identical characteristics in the late 18th and 19th centuries, the international context in which it was situated was radically different in the two periods. Hence the significance of the phenomenon was also different: if, in the late 18th century, it had represented a tendency to hierarchical order guaranteeing universal peace ($N^+ \rightarrow S^-$), at the end of the 19th century, it rather expressed a tendency to universal anarchy and war ($N^- \rightarrow S^+$). It is in this sense that the English imperialism of Hobson's time represented only the 'ghost' and not the 'reality' of formal imperialism – its reality was something quite different, namely 'the theory and the practice of competing empires'. That this was the dominant feature of the epoch is revealed by the sharp rise in English military expenditure: according to data provided by Hobson,[33] this grew from £27.9m in 1884 to £69.8m in 1900 and, after a leap during the Boer War, to £100.8m in 1903. The public debt soared at the same pace, throwing into crisis the whole edifice of free trade:

> Government loans for direct enterprise largely connected with armament and communications rose from zero before 1870 to around £50 million just before the First World War. It was this rather than the negligible expenditure on social welfare (other than education) which made the old policy of cheap and inactive government impossible.[34]

The policy of free trade was frequently called into question in government circles, but Chamberlain's electoral defeat in 1908 kept it formally alive for another decade. At the same time, however, territorial expansionism and militarism had irreversibly exacerbated inter-state relations, producing that situation of anarchy which would very soon result in the First World War and the subsequent abandonment of free trade for ever.

This configuration of events, in which international rivalry was progressively transposed from the plane of relations between individuals of different nationalities to that of inter-state relations, had its roots in the near-complete informal empire of free trade, which, as we have seen, was established towards the end of the 1860's. For free circulation of commodities, labour and capital had stimulated a shift in the international division of labour, tending to divest England of its 'naturally' hegemonic position as the 'workshop of the world':

> In the literal sense Britain was perhaps never the 'workshop of the world', but her industrial dominance was such in the middle of the

[33] Hobson, op. cit., p. 65.
[34] Hobsbawm, op. cit., p. 202.

nineteenth century that the phrase is legitimate. . . . The chief rival state, even then, was the USA – or rather the northern states of the USA – with France, the German Confederation and Belgium. All these, except in part little Belgium, lagged behind British industrialization, but it was already clear that if they and others continued to industrialize, Britain's advantage would inevitably shrink. And so it did. . . . [By] 1870 the 'workshop of the world' possessed only between one quarter and one fifth of the world's steam power, and produced much less than half its steel. By the end of the 1880s the relative decline was visible even in the formerly dominant branches of production. By the early 1890s the USA and Germany both passed Britain in the production of the crucial commodity of industrialization, steel. From then on Britain was one of a group of great industrial powers, but not the leader of industrialization. Indeed, among the industrial powers it was the most sluggish and the one which showed most obvious signs of relative decline.[35]

From 1873 onwards, the decline of England's 'natural' monopoly proceeded in a context of acute international rivalry, which provoked a long and precipitate fall in the prices obtained by English exports: although their volume increased, their value stagnated for nearly twenty years, producing a sharp and growing balance-of-payments deficit. In this situation, England's adherence to free trade came more and more to depend on its ability to close the trade gap with revenue of another kind. Of primary importance in this respect were the returns on investment abroad. But here too, the industrialization of other countries was beginning to make itself felt: continental Europe and the USA, which in the 1860's had absorbed more than a half of English foreign investment, attracted in the 1880's less than a third.

Thus, in order to maintain its own free-trade policy, England came increasingly to depend on the proceeds of investment in less developed areas, which, while geographically more extensive, were economically more restricted. Latin America, and above all the Dominions, replaced Europe and the United States as the privileged sites of English investment, absorbing nearly a half of the total in the 1880's, as against less than a

[35] Ibid., p. 110.

quarter in the 1860's. However, by itself, and thus in the long term, this 'base' could not support the weight of a growing trade deficit as well as provide a surplus for new investment. Either these regions would undergo effective development, in which case the outlets for English foreign investment would shrink still further; or else they would not develop, and it would become difficult to recover the money invested in them.

As we know, the former tendency was to prevail in the Dominions, the latter in the 'honorary' Dominions of Latin America. In either case, towards the end of the century the onus of correcting the English trade deficit and providing an excess for new investment was gradually shifted from foreign investment income to the *tribute* drawn from the provinces of the formal empire, above all India:

> The surplus in India's trade with the rest of the world rose in the latter half of the century from £4 million to £50 million. This second surplus was earned not with Britain, but with the USA, Western Europe and Japan from sales of cotton and jute, and later of textile manufactures also. At the same time, Britain continued to export more to India than she imported from India. British exporters found a market in India for textiles, sheet steel and other products that were being challenged in other markets. In addition to the direct-trade balance, Britain's balance of payments with India was augmented by receipts from the 'Home Charges' – for the British administration – and from interest on the Indian Government debt (which rose from £70 million to £225 million in the last quarter of the century). The resulting surplus had risen by 1910 to over £60 million. Thus not only the funds for investment in India itself but a large part of the total investment-income from overseas, that gave Britain her balance of payments surplus in the last quarter of the nineteenth century, was provided by India.[36]

To conclude, the decline of England's 'natural' monopoly as 'workshop of the world' reinforced the role played by India as 'the exception which proved the rule' of free trade (§10). But the exception also tended to become the rule: we should not be deceived by the fact that expansion of the English State beyond its national boundaries took place in the name of free trade.

[36] Barratt Brown, op. cit. (1963), pp. 84–5.

Here too, the characteristic tendencies of the preceding epoch were subsumed under the newly-emerging tendencies, without however determining their significance. This was defined by the convergence of English expansionist policy ($N^- \rightarrow S^+$) with that of other rising powers ($NS \rightarrow S^+$), leading towards a new situation of anarchy and universal war.

12. We have now succeeded in locating with some precision *the object of Hobson's discourse*. In the opening pages of his *Study*, he sought to determine the significance (i.e., the importance) of the concept of imperialism of his time, by drawing a number of distinctions and oppositions. These have allowed us to define a conceptual grid (§6) capable of ordering, synchronically and diachronically, the multiplicity of events and tendencies that can be ranged under the generic denomination of imperialism. In the process, we have identified four distinct, and in some respects antithetical, meanings which may be attributed to the term or signifier in question, indeed which were in practice assumed by it during the two-and-a-half centuries of English world hegemony.

In other words, the meaning of the concept of imperialism has repeatedly changed. It is precisely the capacity of Hobson's grid (represented in Fig. 8) to define the *direction* of these changes which makes it scientifically more valid than that represented by Fig. 3 and implicit in the conventional historiographical critique of his positions. The contrast between these two representations is a token of the poverty of historiography when it claims to invalidate the propositions of a theory merely by pointing to facts which the theory cannot and does not seek to embrace.

The essential correctness of Hobson's judgment was very soon demonstrated by the outbreak of the First World War, which led to England's first open break with the principles and the practice of free trade. In order to finance the war effort, the English government introduced in 1915 a series of duties, later retained as protective customs, on durable consumer goods. It is true that in the 1920's a last vain attempt was made to restore at least the semblance of the informal empire of free trade, but it had no other effect than to make even more dramatic the definitive breakdown of the 1930's.

> In the early thirties, change set in with abruptness. Its landmarks were the abandonment of the gold standard by Great Britain; the Five-Year Plans in Russia; the launching of the New Deal; the National Socialist Revolution in Germany; the collapse of the League in favour of autarchist empires. While at the end of the Great War nineteenth century ideals were paramount, and their influence dominated the following decade, by 1940 every vestige of the international system had disappeared and, apart from a few enclaves, the nations were living in an entirely new international setting.[37]

The collapse of the gold standard was the central event of this process. International trade was deprived of a universally accepted means of payment and took on barter-like forms, subject to detailed state mediation. Economic competition between individuals and firms of different nationalities became a phenomenon wholly internal to political rivalry among their respective states – a rivalry which progressively rose until it overflowed in the Second World War.

In this situation, England appeared at the mercy of events: not a trace remained of its hegemonic position, of its capacity to impose a code of conduct on the international system. Even when it formally abandoned free-trade policies, it suffered rather than determined the actions of others:

> It was not until the slump of 1931 finally destroyed the single web of world trading and financial transactions whose centre was London and the pound sterling, that Free Trade went. Even then it was not Britain that abandoned it. It was the world that abandoned London.[38]

The only recourse left was to cultivate tighter relations with the Dominions and with the provinces of a formal empire that had grown enormously in the last phase of England's hegemony.

---

[37] K. Polanyi, *The Great Transformation*, Boston 1944, p. 23.
[38] Hobsbawm, op. cit., p. 207.

At the Ottawa Conference in 1932, a system of customs duties was elaborated, the so-called imperial preferences, which discriminated in favour of exchanges within the empire, thereby accentuating the developing trend of 'vertical' trade flows (between centre and periphery of opposed empires) to the detriment of 'horizontal' exchange (between sovereign and independent nation-states), which was ever more rigidly regulated by bilateral agreements.

Analogous tendencies manifested themselves in the movement of men and capital. England's indebtedness during the First World War had already compelled it to liquidate the greater part of its investments in the United States. Then, in the inter-war period, English investments in Latin America were progressively supplanted by American capital, while in general recuperation of capital invested outside the borders of the empire became more and more problematic. This resulted in a dramatic fall in English foreign investment (from 9.3% of national income in the period 1910–13, to 1.6% in 1925–29, and −1.3% in 1935–39) and a sharp rise in such investment within the safe confines of the empire (59% in 1930 against 47% in 1913). The growing restrictions imposed on the international movement of labour in this period, and the corresponding reinforcement of economic links between centre and periphery of the empires, also restructured the flow of migration along vertical lines. The closely-woven net of informal ties, which had connected the nations to one another about the middle of the 19th century, facilitating their expansion through mutual 'crossing', disintegrated. National economies became relatively watertight compartments.

The British empire was the most extensive of these compartments; but it was now a reality in contraction. England seemed to be retracing the path on which it had entered in the second half of the 17th century, when its rise to world hegemony had begun. The last act of its retreat was played out after the Second World War, when England's second 'colonial' empire disintegrated and the English State returned within its national boundaries.

This withdrawal may be represented, in the conceptual space

Fig. 9

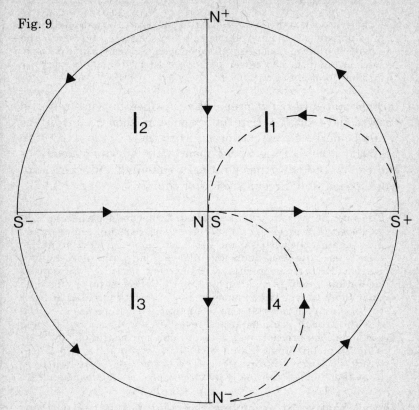

defined in previous sections, by means of an arc $S^+ \to NS$, such
as that now dotted in Fig. 9. The position of this arc within the
space I_1 is justified by the fact that, as we shall see in the next
chapter, imperialism assumed a fresh 'nationalist' significance
in the first half of this century. For the moment, however, we
are concerned only to contrast this course with the alternative
that Hobson indicated for England. In fact, he offered no
alternative to the decline of English hegemony – only an alternative form of decline: a conscious and voluntary abandonment of the country's role as a great power. Only in this way
would it be possible to realize 'the fundamental conception
upon which nineteenth-century Free Trade prematurely
relied':

> If there is one condition precedent to effective internationalism or to establishment of any reliable relations between States, it is the existence of strong, secure, well-developed, and responsible nations. Internationalism can never be subserved by the suppression or forcible adoption of nations.[39]

If other states were not prepared to co-operate peacefully and entered the road of territorial expansion, then no advantage would be derived from competing with them in the attempt to keep the 'doors' of the world open to one's own commodities and capital. Only further political weakening and a threat to world peace would result from that course:

> The 'open door' is an advantage to our trade, but not a necessity. If we have to spend vast sums and incur vast risks in keeping 'doors open' against the wishes of our best customers, it is more profitable to let them close these doors and take our gain by the more indirect but equally certain process of roundabout trade. . . . These considerations ought to make us willing that other nations should do their share of expansion and development, well contented to await the profit which must accrue to us from every increase of world-wealth through ordinary processes of exchange. . . . Since these other nations are not only eager to do their share, but by their jealousy at our undertaking their work continually threaten to wreck the peace of Europe, it seems sheer madness for Great Britain to weaken herself politically by further process of expansion.[40]

The alternative to expanding the State beyond its national boundaries was, for Hobson, a policy of intensive development of human and natural resources within the nation, as a necessary premise of effective internationalism:

> Everywhere the issue of quantitative versus qualitative growth comes up. This is the entire issue of empire. . . . A nation may either, following the example of Denmark or Switzerland, put brains into agriculture, develop a finely varied system of public education, general and technical, apply the ripest science to its special manufacturing industries, and so support in progressive comfort and character a considerable population upon a strictly limited area;

[39] Hobson, op. cit., pp. 362–3.
[40] Ibid., pp. 68–70.

or it may, like Great Britain, neglect its agriculture, allowing its lands to go out of cultivation and its population to grow up in towns, fall behind other nations in its methods of education and in its capacity of adapting to its uses the latest scientific knowledge, in order that it may squander its pecuniary and military resources in forcing bad markets and finding speculative fields of investment in distant corners of the earth, adding millions of square miles and of unassimilable population to the area of the Empire.[41]

In other words, Hobson was proposing that England should anticipate the time of its inevitable decline as a great power, to avoid exacerbating politico-military rivalry between states by defence of its own hegemonic position, and to prepare the conditions of effective internationalism within its own national boundaries. This alternative path may be designated by an arc $N^- \to NS$, such as that just dotted in Fig. 9. Its 'terminus' is thus the same as that of the arc $N^- \to S^+ \to NS$, which designates the path actually travelled by England. But the conceptual space separating the two corresponds to the half-century of international anarchy manifested in, among other things, two World Wars – precisely the events that Hobson feared. It is this difference that, in the last analysis, shows us the significance (that is, the importance) of Hobson's concept of imperialism.

[41] Ibid., pp. 92–3.

3.

The Reduplication

Trajectories of US and German Imperialism

13. The outbreak of the First World War and the events of the next thirty years revealed all the importance of Hobson's concept of imperialism. Precisely for that reason they could no longer be understood within its framework. In the terms defined in Figs. 8 and 9, once the tendencies designated by $NS \to S^+$ manifested themselves, imperialism lost its significance I_4 to assume another. In this chapter, I shall attempt to demonstrate in what sense and to what extent the succession, nationalist imperialism (I_1), formal imperialism (I_2), informal imperialism (I_3), imperialism *tout court* (I_4), which characterized the two-and-a-half centuries of English world hegemony, has been repeated – or reduplicated – from the beginning of the 20th century up to this day.

Before we proceed, however, this is a good point at which to explain how the various powers involved in the struggle for world hegemony were already 'bearers' of diverse significations of imperialism at the end of the last century. Hobson left the latter in the shade in order to illuminate the particular image which interested him. But today we can and must bring them into focus.

In particularly sharp relief stands the 'nationalist' character of German imperialism, which was in certain respects the direct and immediate projection of the Prussian expansionism that led to the political unification of Germany. As in the case of 17th-century English imperialism, it would have been difficult, without the benefit of hindsight, to say where nationalism ended and imperialism began: for instance, Cromwell's bloody

reconquest of Ireland, which served as a prelude to the Navigation Acts and the wars with Holland – was that still nationalism
or already imperialism? Similarly, what was the nature of the
Prussian conquest of Alsace-Lorraine in 1871? Like England
two-and-a-half centuries earlier, late 19th century Germany
was a 'late-comer', aspiring to a redivision of the world which
would create the 'living space' (*Lebensraum*) necessary for the
expansion of its own nationality:

> Having no significant overseas possessions . . . and feeling hemmed
> in at home, [the Germans] came to rest their hopes on the idea of
> Central European hegemony. From there it was only a step to the
> idea of 'colonizing' the Slavs: the Ukraine was to be their Africa.
> In this respect, Hitler was merely the executor of a Pan-German
> programme which had begun to take shape in the 1890s.[42]

This strategic vision called for control of the Balkans and the
Middle East, in opposition to the expansionist goals of Russia.
By the end of the 1890's, moreover, Germany was in a position
to challenge British naval supremacy, and thus to end its
reliance on England's good-will for the realization of its plans
of continental hegemony: 'Without naval power Germany's
position in the world resembles that of a shell-fish without a
shell,' wrote Tirpitz, the initiator of the German naval pro-
gramme adopted at the beginning of this century.

In other words, Germany set out to retread the militarist and
colonialist path which had carried England to world hegemony
in the second half of the 17th century; and just as the earlier
attempt had brought England into conflict with Holland, so did
Germany enter into direct contradiction with England.

Quite different was the significance of the imperialism borne
by the other great rising power of the late 19th century: the
United States. Although it too was a late-comer, the USA had
already solved its *Lebensraum* problem in the first half of the
19th century – a problem which had loomed large in the ideology of the North American colonists before Independence.
Thus, Franklin 'predicted that the population of the colonies

---

[42] Lichtheim, op. cit., p. 67.

would double every quarter century and admonished the British Government to secure additional living space for these newcomers, on the grounds that a prince who "acquires new Territory, if he finds it vacant, or removes the Natives to give his own People Room" deserves the gratitude of posterity'.[43]

Freed from English imperial control, the young United States threw itself into almost boundless territorial growth at the expense of the native populations and the other colonial peoples of America (French and Spanish). To the north, the conquest of Canada was blocked by the English in 1812; but to the south and east, expansion seemed to have no limits: between 1803 and 1853, the USA acquired or conquered from the declining colonial powers (France and Spain) or from newly-emerging Latin American nations about 2.3 million square miles – as much again as it possessed at the beginning of the period. The limits to expansion were more internal than external: once they had reached the Caribbean coast, the Southern states were in favour of annexing Cuba as a new slave territory. But they encountered the firm opposition of the Northern states, which feared a change in the relationship of forces between the free states and the slave states.

This was one aspect of the growing internal conflict which would very soon result in the Civil War (1860–65). The victory of the North marked the end of territorial expansion. Thus when in the second half of the 19th century a race for territorial annexation began between the other powers, the United States had already completed one. As Stedman Jones has noted:

> American historians who speak complacently of the absence of the settler-type colonialism characteristic of European powers merely conceal the fact that the whole *internal* history of United States imperialism was one vast process of territorial seizure and occupation. The absence of territorialism 'abroad' was founded on an unprecedented territorialism 'at home'.[44]

---

[43] Ibid., p. 58.
[44] G. Stedman Jones, 'The History of US Imperialism', in R. Blackburn (ed.) *Ideology in Social Science*, London 1972, pp. 216–7. Emphasis in the original.

This 'internalization' of imperialism also manifested itself at an ideological level. The idea of 'empire' had in fact dominated American political thought since the very beginning, and the goal of the War of Independence itself had been to form an empire which would allow greater autonomy to the American colonies:

> To both of the political parties – Federalists and Republicans – the new federal union was an empire. The two terms were equivalents in the vocabularies of Washington, Adams, Hamilton, and Jefferson.[45]

After the Civil War, the term empire was avoided and replaced by 'nation'. No doubt this reflected a concern to take a distance from the connotations of decadence which the term was assuming in Europe. But it expressed perhaps still more the fact that a North American continental empire had already been created with the subordination of the Southern states, and that the principal objective now was to forge it into a single nation.

At any event, American expansionism changed course decisively in the three decades following the Civil War. Internally, 'colonization' of the acquired territories proceeded at an intense pace (the railway systems were completed, and farmers, cattle-breeders and speculators occupied more land in these thirty years than had been occupied in the three previous centuries). Externally, the United States embarked upon a path of informal-type expansionism. This is not to say that no further annexations occurred. In fact, Alaska was acquired in 1867; and although Secretary of State Seward was prevented by a Senate veto from taking concrete steps to incorporate the Hawaian Islands, he managed all the same to annex the Midway Islands, 1,200 miles further to the east. After the integration of Alaska (which sandwiched British Columbia between American territories) there were even plans to step up the pressure on Canada to become part of the United States. But

---

[45] R. W. Van Alstyne, *The American Empire: Its Historical Pattern and Evolution*, Routledge 1960, p. 10.

the importance of these annexations, and of others such as Panama which were starting to be prospected, no longer consisted in the geographical extent of colonization. They were rather inserted in a strategy of informal domination of the Pacific, protected in the north by Alaska, in the centre by Hawaii and California, and in the south by control of Panama, to guarantee the free circulation of American commodities and capital.[46]

In the closing decades of the 19th century, the United States came more and more to complement, and in part to replace, England as the centre of the informal empire of free trade. We shall see later (§16) that in important respects the American 'open-door' policy always differed from that of the English – for instance, the United States never became a free-trade power in the sense that England had been one. For the moment, however, we are concerned simply to register the fact the United States became only marginally an imperialist power, in the sense exhibited by the principal European States at the turn of the century.

This judgment would seem to conflict with the evidence of a sharp rise in American naval expenditure in the 1890's, the war against Spain at the end of the decade and of the subsequent occupation of the Panama Canal Zone. Of course, there is no reason to deny that these events were an integral part of the general tendency of the epoch to greater political rivalry among states. But in this case, not only were they so circumscribed in time that they assumed an almost episodic character, but they were also almost totally homogeneous with the policy of territorial expansion of the previous thirty years. In fact, the Spanish-American war and the occupation of the Panama Canal did no more than realize Seward's strategic project of thirty-five years earlier: the Hawaii Islands were annexed as the base necessary for domination of the Pacific and trade penetration of the Far East; even in the Philippines, all that was initially sought was a suitable naval base – it was the

---

[46] W. A. Williams, *The Contours of American History*, New York 1961, pp. 318 ff.

rebellion against American occupation that rendered annexation an 'unfortunate necessity'.[47]

In any case, the significance of these acquisitions and of the policy of Pacific domination was rapidly clarified by US actions in China. Unlike the English 'open-door' policy, which acknowledged the existence of privileged spheres of interest, the US counterpart specified absolute equality of treatment for the various powers, as well as acceptance of the territorial and administrative integrity of China. This course therefore involved resistance to tendencies which broke up the unity of the world market, and formal support for the nationalist tendencies then beginning to take shape in the non-European world. It was in evidence above all under Wilson, whose political philosophy was in a number of crucial respects similar to that of Hobson. In particular, Wilson's idea of universal peace was inextricably linked to the concept of an informal order, which, while not rigidly free-tradist, was yet based on the freest international circulation of commodities and capital practicable.

The imperialism of the powers emerging at the end of the 19th century thus had a different significance from the English phenomenon we examined in sections 7 and 11. In the terms defined in the last chapter, the imperialism of the newly-emerging powers may be represented by means of the diagram of Fig. 10, where I_1 designates the nationalist imperialism of Germany, and I_3 the informal imperialism of the United States.[48]

More precisely, $NS \rightarrow S^+$ designates German imperialism as a projection of the Prussian expansionism which resulted in the unification of Germany; and $S^+ \rightarrow N^+$ refers to the tendency of

[47] Stedman Jones, op. cit., p. 227.

[48] The definition I am about to give of the imperialism of the newly-emerging powers differs from, but does not contradict, that formulated at the end of the first chapter, when I designated the trajectories of German nationalism by means of $S^- \rightarrow NS \rightarrow S^+$ and that of American nationalism by means of $N^+ \rightarrow NS \rightarrow N^-$ (§6). There, I was abstracting them from the concept of hegemony, which has since allowed me to articulate these two co-ordinates in a single representation capable of univocally defining the imperialism of the hegemonic power. The imperialism of the emerging powers is thus now to be *re*-defined in accordance with this possibility of articulation.

this imperialism to create 'living space' for the expansion of the young German nation. $S^- \to NS$ and $S^- \to N^-$, for their part, designate jointly the divergence of imperialism and nationalism which came to characterize American expansionism after the Civil War: on the one hand, the tendency to forge the North American continental empire into a nation ($S^- \to NS$); on the other hand, the tendency to transform continent-wide formal imperialism into informal imperialism of a universal character ($S^- \to N^-$).

The reader will notice that the diagram of Fig. 10 is the complement of that of Fig. 4. Superimposing the one on the other, we obtain the diagram of Fig. 8, which then permits at

Fig. 10

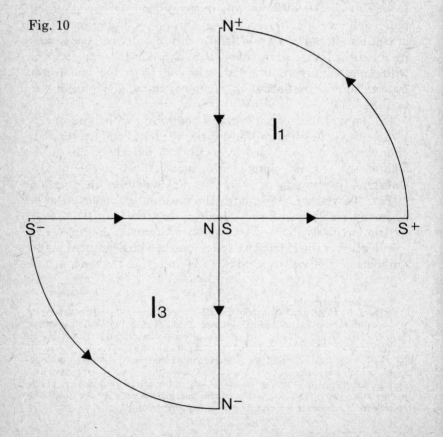

once a synchronic and diachronic reading. The quadrants I_1, I_2, I_3, and I_4 can, that is, just as well designate the series of meanings which English imperialism gradually assumed in its two-and-a-half centuries of world hegemony, as they do the diverse significances simultaneously assumed by imperialism when English hegemony was in decline.

At first sight, the diagram of Fig. 10 indicates that even the imperialism of the newly-emerging powers was not univocal in character – since it could assume opposite meanings (I_1 and I_3). But as the significance of the imperialism of the declining power was in the last analysis determined by $N^- \rightarrow S^+$ and not by $N^+ \rightarrow S^-$ (§7), so Fig. 10 focuses the fact that Hobson's grid defines $S^- \rightarrow N^-$ rather than $S^+ \rightarrow N^+$ as the tendency which ultimately decided the significance of the imperialism of the newly-emerging powers. In effect, the convergence at N^- of the ensembles I_1 and I_3 is less immediate and linear than the convergence at S^+ of the ensembles I_2 and I_4. Unlike the sub-ensemble I_2, the sub-ensemble I_1 does not really imply straightforward convergence at NS, but rather signals a tendency to circularity among nationalist and imperialist phenomena – a tendency represented precisely by the concatenation NS $\rightarrow S^+ \rightarrow N^+ \rightarrow$ NS. . . . We shall see in a moment what historical significance may be attached to this tendency to circularity of nationalist imperialism. But we may already conclude that it can only weaken or delay, and not block, the convergence at N^-.[49]

Hobson's concept of imperialism thus emerges with a yet greater precision. The conscious and voluntary abandonment of a great power role – the trajectory $N^- \rightarrow$ NS in Fig. 9 which Hobson proposed for England as an alternative to inevitable and tragic disintegration of its hegemony ($N^- \rightarrow S^+ \rightarrow$ NS) – would not have resulted in a political vacuum, but would have strengthened the pacifist component of the imperialism of the rising powers. Peaceful replacement of British by US hegemony was, moreover, the substance of American foreign policy

---

[49] If the reader wishes to interpret Fig. 10 as a digraph, then N^- could be regarded as its 'well'.

thinking at the end of the 19th and the beginning of the 20th century. While this vision did not adequately take into account the other – nationalist – component of the imperialism of the rising powers, it is nevertheless also true that territorial expansion of the English state during these years decisively shifted the compass-needle away from peaceful interchange of goods and ideas between firms and individuals of different nationality towards politico-military rivalry among states. Hobson's vision was not, after all, completely lacking in political realism.

14. The path of nationalist imperialism did not lead Germany to a lasting hegemonic position, of the kind that England had captured two hundred years earlier. Such a road to hegemony was largely blocked, both because others had already travelled it, and because the international system had, in the intervening period, been more rigidly structured into nation-states. Germany's quest for hegemony thus ended by unifying old and new powers in a rival bloc against it. England and the United States were alike endangered by Germany's aspirations to domination of the seas; while its drive to continental hegemony constituted a threat to both France and Russia.

As is well known, defeat in the First World War did not change the dimensional structure of German nationalist imperialism, but led to its radicalization. The ideology of 'living space' passed into the doctrine of the *grossdeutsches Reich* – a kind of Germanic 'Monroe Doctrine' which inspired the expansionism and racism of the Nazi State. This radicalization was accompanied by a 'perverse' capacity to exasperate the anarchic tendencies latent in the international system:

> Germany, once defeated, was in a position to recognize the hidden shortcomings of the nineteenth-century order, and to employ this knowledge to speed the destruction of that order. A kind of sinister intellectual superiority accrued to those of her statesmen in the thirties who turned their minds to this task of disruption, which often extended to the development of new methods of finance, trade, war, and social organisation, in the course of their attempt to force matters into the trend of their policies.[50]

[50] Polanyi, op. cit., p. 29.

Germany thus came to enjoy momentary hegemony over the international system – a position which secured it, among other things, the alliance of other late-comers affected by problems of 'living space' (Japan and Italy).[51] This hegemony did not last long. Grouped together in an alliance, the expansionist tendencies which had developed independently within the three Axis nation-states reinforced one another, driving great powers whose own aspirations to hegemony were threatened and nation-states whose very survival was in jeopardy, into a common front against them.

In other words, German nationalist imperialism of the first half of this century, instead of representing the first phase of a new hegemony, as had been the case with English nationalist imperialism in the 17th and 18th centuries, tended to chase its own tail, so to speak, unleashing a vicious circle of nationalism and imperialism. These two routes, expressed within the conceptual space which we have defined as 'nationalist imperialism', are represented in Fig. 11 by means of an arc $NS \rightarrow N^+$ and a circle inscribed in the quadrant I_1, respectively. As we saw in section 8, the former designates the path which brought England to lasting world hegemony in the 18th century; the latter designates the vicious circle in which Germany became caught when, in the first half of the 20th century, it attempted to retread this path in a radically changed geo-political situation.

Beyond these two differences, however, there is an evident analogy between the two phases of nationalist imperialism: not only from the point of view of their 'origin' (the process of formation of a nation-state) and their 'function' (the creation of space for expanding the nationality), but also from that of their 'outcomes', or rather, of the conditions under which they were superseded. Thus, the new period of world-wide anarchy and

[51] The level of abstraction involved in the present investigation allows of no differentiation among the imperialisms of the three Axis powers, in particular Germany and Japan, which pursued the path of nationalist imperialism with greatest success, however temporarily. Despite the profound differences between the socio-political structures of these two countries (cf. K. Hayashi, 'Japan and Germany in the Interwar Period' in J. W. Morley, ed., *Dilemmas of Growth in Prewar Japan*, Princeton 1971) the two imperialisms can be represented in an identical way within our grid.

Fig. 11

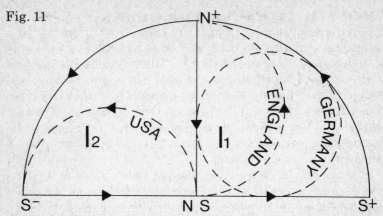

war also ended by generating nationalist tendencies in the colonial world, as a result of which nationalist imperialism was superseded as the dominant form of international relations.

In this case too there is a clear link between the mobilization of the colonies and provinces of the rival empires for war, and the development within them of national liberation movements. Just as the mobilization of the North American colonies had fostered their nationalist sentiments, so did the Second World War mark a dramatic turn in the affirmation of nationalism within the new colonial world:

> By the end of the war a number of indestructible realities had been created. The most significant of these was not the reversal of the relationship between debtors and creditors, nor even the Atlantic and UN Charters and other events and agreements which ratified and set the seal upon national sovereignty, nor the abolition of treaties of capitulation, extra-territorial rights and racial discrimination. In most cases, all these things could be, and would be, renounced and annulled. . . . Of greater importance was the fact that the colonial peoples were taking up arms against the aggressors, having already done their duty for the common victory as regular soldiers and sailors, as workers in the arms and transport industries, and as fighters in the national liberation armies.[52]

The analogy should nevertheless be treated with some caution, since, with only a few exceptions (e.g., South Africa) it was not

[52] W. Markov, *Sistemi Coloniali e Movimenti di Liberazione*, Rome 1961, p. 69.

the settlers but the colonized peoples who broke away from the metropolis to form new nation-states. In effect, so far as relations between colonized and colonizers are concerned, the use of a single term 'colonial revolution' conceals realities which differ radically according to whether the former or the latter are its subject. But the 'colonial revolution' interests us here exclusively from the point of view of its impact upon nation-states struggling for world hegemony; and in this sense, it is perfectly legitimate to employ a single designation $(N^+ \rightarrow NS)$ both for the nationalist tendencies in the colonial arenas of the late 18th century and for those of the mid-20th century.

Moreover, this was the standpoint adopted by Lenin when he included Boer nationalism within the anti-imperialist movements of the colonial world. Indeed, it seems to me that the ensemble I_1 was precisely the object of which Lenin was speaking. For him, as for Hobson, imperialism was above all a tendency to universal war resulting from the expansion of states beyond their national boundaries $(NS \rightarrow S^+)$. However, although he adopted Hobson's definition of imperialism as 'anarchy and war' in opposition to the traditional connotation of 'hierarchy and peace', Lenin was writing at a time when the tendency in question had already clearly manifested itself with the outbreak of the First World War, and when imperialism was starting to assume a different significance from that which Hobson had ascribed to it (L_4).

Lenin's fundamental insight was precisely his stress on the tendency of imperialism to generate national liberation movements, and his perception that this tendency constituted the limit, *at the level of international relations*, of the imperialism of his epoch:

> The imperialist war . . . contributed to the growth of the revolutionary movement, because the European imperialists had to enlist whole colonial regiments in their struggle. The imperialist war aroused the East also and drew its peoples into international politics. Britain and France armed colonial peoples and helped them to familiarize themselves with military technique and up-to-date machines. That knowledge they will use against the imperialist gentry. The period of the awakening of the East in the contemporary

revolution is being succeeded by a period in which all the Eastern peoples will participate in deciding the destiny of the whole world, so as not to be simply objects of the enrichment of others. The peoples of the East are becoming alive to the need for practical action, for every nation to take part in shaping the destiny of all mankind.[53]

Thus, both Hobson and Lenin spoke of the tendency to anarchy and universal war ($NS \rightarrow S^+$). But whereas the former referred to it as a component of the ensemble L_4, that is as the outcome of ongoing tendencies, the latter spoke of it as a component of the ensemble I_1, that is as a premise of the development of national liberation movements in the colonies.

15. In the same way as the outbreak of the First World War and the events of the next thirty years demonstrated the importance of Hobson's concept of imperialism, yet surpassed its meaning, so the new wave of nationalism released since the Second World War demonstrated the enormous importance of Lenin's concept of imperialism, while by that very token transcending its meaning. After the last war, in fact, the nature of the struggle for hegemony among the great powers underwent radical alteration; and this change has, in its turn, remoulded the national liberation movements themselves.

As is well known, the Second World War not only unleashed a new wave of nationalism, but also signalled the assertion of almost total American economic and military predominance:

If before the war America's economy was one among other great economies, after the war it became the central economy in a rapidly developing world economy. If before the war America's military had only sporadic significance in the world's conflicts, after the war its nuclear umbrella backed by high technology conventional forces terrorized one part of the world and gave security to the other. Above all, the once loosely jointed federal government of the US became a powerful, wealthy, and stable state, the axis on which much of the world's politics, including those of America's enemies, revolved.[54]

[53] V. I. Lenin, 'Address to the Second All-Russia Congress of Communist Organisations of the Peoples of the East' (Nov. 1919), in *Selected Works*, op. cit., Vol. 3, p. 305.
[54] F. Schurmann, *The Logic of World Power*, New York 1974, p. XXX.

Like the new 'colonial revolution', this American pre-eminence was in a certain sense the result of the previous thirty years of world-wide anarchy and war. The 'domestic territorialism' of the first half of the 19th century, together with the industrial revolution of the second half, had in reality allowed the United States to become by the beginning of this century not only the technologically most advanced, but also the most self-sufficient national economy in the world. What for the other late-comers was only a pervasive aspiration of their ideology and politics, was for the USA a quite 'natural' objective fact. The efforts of these late-comers to redivide the world into self-sufficient empires of a continental character could not but favour those which already constituted such an 'empire' – the United States and, to a lesser extent, the Soviet Union.

During the previous phase of imperialism, the tendencies to colonial revolution and affirmation of American hegemony had developed in parallel, exhibiting in certain respects common objectives. In the situation existing at the end of the last century, for example, the demand that China's territorial and administrative integrity be maintained (§13) was tantamount to an act of support for the nationalist tendencies which were gradually developing in that country, in opposition to the policy of partition or annexation of the sub-continent preferred by the European powers. An analogous role was played by the United States in Latin America, where the application of the Monroe Doctrine had effectively contained European expansionist tendencies. It is true that American policy in this area already prefigured, by its intimidating acts of intervention, the limits of its support for national sovereignty. But that did not stop the USA from presenting itself as an anti-colonialist power faithful to its image of the 'first ex-colony', or from being perceived as such on the world arena.

The United States was thus able to pose during the Second World War as the natural ally of the emergent nationalism in the colonial empires, and as the guarantor of the promises of self-determination and national independence through which the colonial peoples were mobilized against the Axis powers. Immediately after the war, the model of the 'Revolution of 1776' was not merely an American propaganda weapon for use in the colonial world, but also a spontaneous source of inspiration for the colonial peoples themselves. The Democratic Republic of Vietnam, for instance, modelled its 1946 Declaration of Independence on the American document of 1776. In reality, US support, or at least neutrality, in the struggles of the national liberation movements did accelerate the tendency to decolonization in certain areas of particular economic and strategic importance (the Middle-East, India, Indonesia).

Towards the end of the 1940's, however, the nationalist tendencies of the colonial world began to diverge from the expansionist tendencies of the United States – a phenomenon that was to characterize the international arena for more than twenty years. This divarication was to be just one aspect of the form assumed by American hegemony during the period of the so-called Cold War. As was stressed a little earlier, the United States was not the only country to profit from the situation of world-wide anarchy and war which had characterized the first half of the century. To a lesser degree this was also true of Russia – the other nation-state to have, in a certain sense, anticipated and 'internalized' the tendency to territorial annexation of the late 19th century.

Hobson himself noted that Russian expansionism, while falling under the general phenomenon of 'New Imperialism', exhibited a number of specific features which differentiated it from that of the other powers:

Russia . . . stood alone in the character of her imperial growth, which differed from other Imperialisms in that it was principally Asiatic in its achievements and proceeded by direct extension of imperial boundaries, partaking to a larger extent than in the other cases of a regular colonial policy of settlement for purposes of agriculture and industry. It is, however, evident that Russian expansion, though of a more normal and natural order than that which characterizes the new Imperialism, came definitely into competition with the claims and aspirations of the latter in Asia, and was advancing rapidly during the period which is the object of our study.[55]

[55] Hobson, op. cit., pp. 21–2.

Thus Russia had also unexpectedly attained those continental dimensions which were to represent a decisive advantage in the subsequent phase of nationalist imperialism. Unlike the USA, however, Russia did not achieve, at the beginning of the phase in question, those conditions of internal cultural homogeneity and technological superiority which were equally crucial in the assertion of American economic and military pre-eminence. It also occupied a geographical position which exposed it to direct attack from the two most warlike late-comers (Japan to the East, and Germany to the West). Russia was thus to rely principally upon political revolution and ideology in defending its territorial integrity and in creating a *cordon sanitaire* to protect it from external attack.[56]

In this case too, the distinction between nationalism and expansionism is largely arbitrary. One thing is certain, however: at the end of the Second World War, the USSR could represent itself, and be perceived, on the world arena as the bearer of an alternative model of pacification/integration of nationalism, both old and new. Having defeated the nationalist imperialism of the Axis powers, the United States now found in the formal order, of a predominantly political and continental character, of which the Soviet Union was the bearer, a new obstacle to that informal order, of a predominantly economic and global character, of which the US had been the bearer since the end of the 19th century.

This was perhaps the major reason, at the level of international relations, why American economic and military pre-

---

[56] These brief allusions to the dynamic of Russian expansionism necessarily disregard the break between the Tsarist state and the Soviet state – just as our passing remarks on the dynamic of French expansionism after the Seven Years War (§9) placed in the shade the disjuncture represented by the French Revolution of 1789. This is partially due to the fact that the present analysis is restricted to those nation-states (England, Germany and the USA) which have actually won a position of world hegemony during the last three hundred years. The characteristic tendencies of the other nation-states, including the rivals of England and the USA, France and Russia, are only considered in so far as they shed light upon the actions of the hegemonic powers. But even apart from these limits, the plane we have chosen for analysis – that of expansionist tendencies – is perhaps that least suitable for bringing out the medium to long term disjunctures initiated by the social revolutions of 1789 and 1917.

eminence did not lead in the short to medium term to the realization of Wilson's vision of an informal world order, in which American hegemony would be guaranteed by economic superiority and only secondarily by political and military mechanisms. Instead it was Franklin D. Roosevelt's vision, which attached decisive weight to political mediation, which prevailed:

> What Roosevelt wanted was to remake the entire world in the American image, and particularly to repeat for the world what the Americans had done for themselves a century and a half before – to create one out of the many, as the official American motto goes. . . .
>   What died with Roosevelt was the hope that Russia could be woven into the new order, and, eventually, what came into being was a containment policy directed against Russia. But the kind of policies that containment dictated for the free world were essentially those already sketched out in Roosevelt's vision: American military power strategically placed throughout the world, a new monetary system based on the dollar, economic assistance to the destroyed countries, political linkages realized through the UN and other international agencies. By the end of the 1940s, a new American world order had clearly emerged.[57]

The American federal government thus extended the role it had assumed of 'state above states' in relations between the States of the Union, to the whole of the so-called Free World. The *formal* character of this order found expression not only in the growing centralization of principal political, military and financial functions in the hands of the American government, but also in the creation of a stable hierarchy of states operating within the various international bodies created in order to reconstruct the political and economic unity of the Free World. In this hierarchy, the existence of which was often explicitly acknowledged, the summit was invariably occupied by the United States; the intermediary positions by the old and new powers of West Europe and Japan, whose conflicts with one another had dominated the first half of the century and whose respective ranks had been drastically reshaped by the Second World

[57] Schurmann, op. cit., pp. 4–5.

War; and the bottom positions by the peripheral countries of the old formal or informal empires.

The practical and ideological justification of this formal empire (which the American New Left has ironically called the Free World Empire) was the threat to American hegemony posed by the formation of the so-called Communist World under Soviet hegemony. The reality of the danger was quite rapidly demonstrated by the success of the Chinese Revolution and therewith the adherence to the Soviet camp of China – the favoured site of American expansionist designs since the second half of the 19th century.

However, this is not the question that interests us here. For our purposes, it is enough to stress the no less, if not more, hierarchical nature of the internal order of the Communist world. For the coexistence of the two hierarchies (and their politico-ideological counterposition) was to prove 'functional' to world peace. In this sense there is no doubt that the specific and dominant characteristic of the Cold War was its super-session of the international anarchy that had dominated the previous thirty years: despite the radical and violent counter-position of the two 'worlds' on the ideological and cultural levels, inter-state relations were effectively put upon a peaceful footing.

Beyond the substantive differences which we shall have occasion to emphasize below, there was a certain broad analogy between this first phase of the *Pax Americana* and the first phase of the *Pax Britannica*. As England had tried, in the half-century following the Seven Years' War, to formalize the pre-eminence which it had gained during the preceding century of world-wide warfare into an imperial system (§9), so did the United States pursue much the same goal at the end of the Second World War. To the Franco-English 'imperial' dualism corresponded now a Russo-American dualism. Each phase exhibited a tendency for a hierarchical order among states to emerge, conducive to a universal peace. The modes and tempos of its realization differed, but there was no mistaking the trend that found expression during the early 60's in the so-called thaw and the doctrine of peaceful coexistence.

The evidence then seems to warrant the ascription of a formal-imperialist character (I_2), as defined in the last chapter, to post-war American imperialism. To be more precise, the rise of the United States to a hegemonic power ought to be designated by means of an arc NS $\rightarrow$ S$^-$ within the quadrant I_2, like that dotted in Fig. 11. Confirmation that this designation is the most satisfactory of those possible within our grid is provided by the fact that, in this case too, the attempt to instal a hierarchical order among states serving to foster universal peace ended by detonating nationalist tendencies within the imperial world (S$^-$ $\rightarrow$ NS), as a result of which these attempts were themselves surpassed. I am referring to the fresh wave of nationalism, whose epicentre was in South-East Asia, which, from the early 60's onwards, threw into crisis Russo-American efforts to formalize a co-dominion over the world.

Cuba's break with the American empire and the withdrawal of China from the Soviet bloc constituted the decisive moments in the formation of a Third World, comprising the nations which had occupied the lower rungs of the two opposing hierarchies. But it was only in the late 60's, when the inability of the USA to sustain its imperial functions became increasingly evident that the epoch finally came to an end and another one started. As Goran Therborn acutely observed when commenting upon the Tet Offensive:

> *The Cold War was a fundamentally unequal conflict, that was presented and experienced on both sides as being equal.* . . . Fought out as a competitive conflict between the USSR and the USA in Europe, it resulted in the massive political and ideological consolidation of capitalism in the West. *An unequal conflict fought as equal redoubles the inequality.* . . . The contemporary conflict between imperialism and national liberation, of which the war in Vietnam is the principal aspect today, is totally different in structure. *It is a conflict between unequal forces presented and lived as unequal.* . . . The Cold War was a struggle on the same plane between two forces at different levels. The protracted war of a guerrilla army against an imperialist military expedition is the armed expression of a conflict where the inequality of the parties is matched by a struggle on disparate planes – each party fighting on different

terrain. . . . *an unequal struggle waged as unequal equalizes the inequality.*[58]

16. At the end of the 60's, then, the international system entered a new phase, which is characterized precisely by the tendency to decomposition of the formal empires constructed during the previous twenty years ($S^- \rightarrow NS$) and by the attempt of the USA to maintain its own hegemonic position on the basis of an informal dominion ($S^- \rightarrow N^-$). The victory of the Vietnamese Revolution accelerated the transformation of the national sovereignty of Third World states from a purely formal autonomy into real political independence – demonstrated at the level of economic relations by more aggressive intervention in the commodity markets and assertions of control over their natural resources:

> For once, countries in the Third World are actively controlling the terms of their trade with the industrialized world and the returns they get from the powerful multinational corporations, instead of the other way round. . . . Nor does the new economic nationalism stop at attempts to control the prices upon which depend the export incomes and through that the economic livelihood of Third World nations. Action on prices is seen only as one component of a general strategy of securing control over marketing and ultimately production in the resource industries which sustain Third World economies.[59]

horseshit

It is obviously too early to evaluate the chances of success of such a 'broader' strategy. But it seems hard to dispute that the relationship of forces between the Third World and metropolitan states has changed decisively, undermining the structure of past relations of 'unequal exchange'.

The shift is even more evident at the political level, where the new independence of Third World countries is manifested above

[58] G. Therborn, 'From Petrograd to Saigon', *New Left Review*, 48, March–April 1968, pp. 4–6. Emphasis in the original.

[59] Girvan, 'Economic Nationalists vs. Multinational Corporations: Revolutionary or Evolutionary Change?' (IDEP duplicated paper), Dakar 1974.

all in their greater promptitude and capacity to resort to war to regulate their mutual relations and consolidate their fragile national unity. Some may question the autonomy of the military decisions taken by these states and argue that the wars which have broken out in the Third World since 1968 are an expression of the Cold War between East and West. But each of these wars – from Biafra to Bangla Desh, from the Middle East to the Horn of Africa – has generated more intense contradictions within the two empires than between them.

Furthermore, latent contradictions had long since existed between the summits and the intermediary rungs of each hierarchy, and they were continuing to develop *pari passu* with those between the summits and the Third World. In the 1960's, after an ebb associated with the Cold War, nationalist tendencies forcefully re-emerged within each zone. In Eastern Europe, the nationalist revival seemed to be linked with a shift in the balance of forces between the Free World Empire and the Soviet bloc to the advantage of the former. In Western Europe, by contrast, the resurgence of nationalism, centred on Gaullist France, appears to have been associated principally with the enfeeblement of the United States as a state above states. In fact, the escalation of intervention in Vietnam, while disclosing the strategic vulnerability of American technological supremacy, exacerbated the financial weakness of the United States in relation to Europe, which had started to set in for other reasons during the late 50's (§23).

In any case, the crisis of American formal imperialism came to a head between 1968 and 1971 and was in practice acknowledged by the US government itself with its announcement of the inconvertibility of the dollar into gold, its theory of the 'five poles' of the international system, and its military withdrawal from Vietnam. The Watergate scandal and the temporary paralysis of the CIA as an 'imperial' police force have subsequently consolidated this turn in foreign policy and modified the powers of the Executive in US internal affairs.

This is not to say, of course, that the United States has given up world hegemony. On the contrary, the sudden abandonment of formal imperialism in favour of informal imperialism seems

to have given a new lease of life to American paramountcy.
From this point of view, the United States has a decisive advantage over the USSR. The Soviet formal 'empire' was from
the outset, and remains today, based upon mechanisms of an
overtly political (i.e. ideological and military) nature. Ameri- *yes*
can formal imperialism, by contrast, represented a tactical
modification, which never repudiated but rather exalted the
informal imperialist vocation which had characterized the
USA since the beginning of the 20th century. Its financial,
military and ideological dominion was actually oriented in the
immediate post-war period towards the reconstruction of
the economic unity of the Free World, as the sole long-term
guarantee of the reproduction of American hegemony.

With the Bretton Woods Agreement, the various national
currencies once again became convertible into a universally
accepted monetary measure on the basis of a *gold-dollar-
standard*, that is, a gold standard mediated by the dollar. The
Marshall Plan and other forms of aid, token of the role of the
US federal government as a state above states (i.e. an imperial
state), effected a considerable redistribution of monetary and
financial resources from the United States to Europe between
1946 and 1958, by means of which the major national currencies
became more and more freely convertible – with respect not
only to current payments but also to capital accounts.

In the general process of commercial liberalization, priority
was given to intra-European trade, which by 1956 was free of
all quantitative restrictions. Subsequently, while two broad
free-trade areas emerged in Europe with US support (the EEC
in 1957, EFTA in 1959), the member-countries of which pledged
themselves to abolish tariff restrictions, the elimination of
physical quotas was extended to trade between Europe and the
dollar zone. Finally, in 1962, the so-called Dillon Round was
successfully concluded with a 20% reduction in customs duties
on industrial products; further negotiations (the Kennedy
Round) centred on the reduction of US customs duties in exchange for greater liberalization of European agricultural
imports.

Over the following decade, as has already been said, the maintenance by the USA of a formal-imperialist hierarchy aroused nationalist reactions within Europe itself, endangering what economic unification had actually been achieved in the Free World. Resistance to liberalization of EEC agricultural imports stalled the Kennedy Round for a good four years; there was growing opposition to extension of the EEC to the countries of North-Western Europe, advocated by the USA. Instead, the Community accepted the association of ex-colonial (or, at any rate, peripheral) countries of Africa and the Mediterranean basin, in a manner which discriminated in practice against the other metropolitan countries of the Free World. Above all, the dollar's function as an international monetary measure – acquired as a result of the Bretton Woods Agreement – was subjected to renewed discussion and then openly contested.

However, the economic unification of the Western world was henceforth an established reality, which transcended the political will of nation-states. This was particularly evident in the currency realm. At the end of 1967, after four years of negotions within the Group of Ten over the creation of a new and *really* international monetary instrument to supersede both the dollar and gold, an agreement was finally reached on Special Drawing Rights (SDRs). The 'impersonal laws' of the market thereafter asserted themselves with a vengeance. The attempts of nation-states to regain control over liquidity at a national and international level – either through imposing further restrictions on international trade, or through limiting the convertibility of their own currencies, or through competitive raising of interest rates – now merely resulted in a further expansion of the margin of national and international liquidity which escaped their control.

Only by accepting the 'laws' of the market and by subordinating its own economic policy to them, could the United States of America reassert its hegemony over Europe and extend it to the rest of the world. Of major importance in this process were the official devaluation of the dollar against gold in 1971; the inauguration of the system of flexible exchange rates; and the withdrawal of troops from Vietnam. The United States thereby freed itself from the shackles of formal imperialism, which had ended by cramping its military and financial supremacy, in order to exercise its hegemony through market forces. Therewith the *Pax Americana* has entered a second phase, in which the relationship between hegemonic nation-state and the world market is reversed: whereas in the first twenty years after the Second World War American hegemony was the agency whereby the unity of the world market was, albeit partially, reconstituted, during the last decade this unity has been, and still is today, the medium of the reassertion of US world hegemony.

In the 70's, then, we have re-entered a phase of informal imperialism which is, so to speak, the double of 19th-century British informal imperialism. In order to avoid ambiguity, it is as well to anticipate a substantive difference between the *Pax Americana* of today and the *Pax Britannica* of the last century. Although both cases involve an informal empire, which may be designated by the ensemble I_3, the specific characteristic of the contemporary phenomenon is not *free trade* but *free enterprise*.

As a matter of fact, we have already noted (§10) that US policy was never rigidly free-tradist. Even though the 30's witnessed an inversion of the roles of England and America – the former giving up every inclination for free trade, the latter moderating its protectionist ideology – the United States never became a free-trade power in the sense that England had been one at the height of its hegemony. As Michael Barratt Brown among others has pointed out, although the United States assumed the role of a great free-market power, tending to eliminate areas of exploitation to which one power had exclusive access, it never actually applied free-trade principles to its own national market.[60] Even in the 60's, first with the Dillon Round then with the Kennedy Round, the United States entered into *negotiations* to liberalize its foreign trade, but did not take *unilateral measures* such as England had done in the 1840's when it repealed the Corn Laws and the Navigation Acts.

The dominant preoccupation of US foreign policy, above all since the Second World War, has been to guarantee the freest

---

[60] Barratt Brown, op. cit. (1963), pp. 205–6.

possible international circulation not so much of commodities as of entrepreneurial activity. Of course, as we shall see in the next chapter, once free international circulation of entrepreneurial activity reaches a given threshold, it needs a certain degree of free trade. But the relationship between the two 'freedoms' is not a rigid one, and the development of international circulation of entrepreneurial activity may be, and in fact has been, furthered by protectionist measures of one kind or another (§22).

In any case, the empire of free enterprise corresponds, like that of free trade, to the essential characteristics of Hobson's image of informal internationalism/imperialism. Quite apart from the fact that, in the medium to long term, free international circulation of entrepreneurial activity develops solid bases for free trade, it promotes in the short term, to a much greater extent than free trade, that expansion through the 'crossing' of various nationalities, and that strengthening of their economic interdependence and cultural homogeneity, which Hobson regarded as the very essence of internationalism (§5).

17. In little more than half a century (from the outbreak of the First World War to the end of the 60's) the significance of imperialism has thus 'traversed' a conceptual space $(I_1 + I_2)$, the passage of which had in other times (from the passing of the Navigation Acts to the 1820's) taken more than a century and a half. For slightly less than a decade, then, imperialism has been gradually reassuming the guise of informal imperialism (I_3); and given the speed at which events now seem to unfold, it is tempting to conclude that we are now rapidly heading for a new phase of imperialism – in the specific sense (I_4) that Hobson attached to the term – destined in its turn to result in a period of world-wide anarchy and war.

It is no accident that recent years have witnessed a revival, at times critical and at times apologetic, of early 20th-century theories of imperialism. In its most fanciful form, the reduplication of Hobson's and Lenin's theory of imperialism predicts the approach of the fateful '1984', described by George Orwell in the novel of the same name. Thus, Samir Amin, in a recent work, has argued that the centralization of capital 'will abolish the modalities of competition that we still know – i.e., monopolistic competition – in order to replace them by direct conflict between states. The phenomenon already discernible and described as the military-monopoly complex would become essential to economic life.'[61]

The projection is usually associated with the decline of US world supremacy and the rise of a certain Soviet hegemony ('In 1984 . . . we shall be drawing closer to the Soviet mode') – an outlook which conflicts with the apparent recovery of the United States after the crisis of the late 60's. Amin does not actually deny that American hegemony has recently been re-affirmed; but he attributes a purely contingent significance to this, linked to the weakness of those who called it into question:

> The successes achieved by the United States . . . in the last few months, both in the Near East and in Europe, should not give rise to any illusions. Neither Gaullism in Europe, nor Nasserism in the Near East represented a serious challenge to the US hegemony over the world system of the last twenty-five years; they were only the first signs of such a challenge, significant at the level of verbal declarations, but insignificant in actuality. The American successes therefore testify more to the weakness and inconsistency of these verbal adversaries than to the real power of the United States. We are convinced that inter-imperialist contradictions will sharpen in the future and that, for this reason, the present international order is doomed.[62]

According to this picture, as American hegemony declines, so will international rivalry grow more acute and shift once again from the level of economic relations among firms of different nationalities to that of political relations among states. The imperialism of the hegemonic power will come to assume the significance I_4, and the 'circle' $S^+ \to N^+ \to S^- \to N^-$ will for the second time close at the point of convergence S^+.

This view seems to me rather hurried. Not that I could rule out the eventuality that the system will move, in the next ten or

[61] S. Amin. 'Une crise structurelle', in Amin et al., *La Crise de l'Imperialisme*, Paris 1975, pp. 25–6.
[62] Ibid., pp. 32–3.

twenty years, towards a period of politicization of international relations, heading in the direction of anarchy in inter-state relations and a new world war. On the contrary, that is certainly possible – and, if we are sufficiently determined, we may also find harbingers of this trend among everyday events. But if we simply take into account the *major* processes of our age – those which are often neglected precisely because of their general character – and if we attempt to order them by means of the grid we have been elaborating, then we shall soon realize that imperialism is for the moment firmly 'anchored' in the significance I_3.[63]

Among these crucial processes, the most important seems to be one mentioned a number of times in previous sections: namely, the renewed domination of so-called market forces over the international system. Beginning in 1968, the year of the uncontrolled explosion of the monetary crisis, the market has reasserted itself as the necessary mediation of inter-state relations, thus marking a 180° turn in comparison with the 30's, when every form of international circulation of money, goods and capital required the mediation of inter-state relations, which were mostly bilateral. In the last few years it has been precisely by exploiting the mediation of the market, and adapting it to their own needs that certain nation-states have strengthened themselves at the expense of others: not only the USA, which has reinforced its hegemonic position by largely marginalizing the Soviet Union in the Third World; but also West Germany, which seems to be taking its revenge on England, the great free-trade power that obstructed Teutonic aspirations to European hegemony at the beginning of the century; and, above all, that dense cluster of nation-states which, endowed with reserves of industrial raw materials, now seeks to supplant their one-time 'colonizers' in economic and political power.

This all-round convulsion of the relationship of forces between states is itself conducive to the development of tensions in those areas where nationalism has a weak political

[63] The advent of the 'Carter era' seems to confirm our evaluation.

Reaganism: a parody of political-
military character of '40s–'50s
line-drawing (Grenada) - an
atavism
Volker: the market hegemon

base, and inter-state conflict may thus play an important role
in forging the internal cohesion of new nations. The wars
issuing from such clashes belong, however, not to the processes
of imperialism, but to those of nationalism. In the same way as
the golden age of the informal empire of free trade was, in certain areas, dominated by wars of unification and national
independence (in Germany and Italy, as well as in America
during the Civil War) so it is quite likely that the golden age of
the informal empire of free enterprise will continue to be
dominated, in areas such as Africa and the Arab world, by wars
for the consolidation or formation of new national units.

조선 ??

The search in every case of local warfare for a clash 'by proxy'
between opposing empires may serve a political purpose, but it
seems to me to have very limited scientific validity. These wars
are rather an expression of the progressive disintegration
$(S^- \rightarrow NS)$ of the hierarchical inter-state structures which
characterized the world system for over twenty years; and in all
probability their effects will tend to converge with the consolidation of the informal empire of free enterprise inscribed in
the policy of the hegemonic power $(S^- \rightarrow N^-)$.

18. Paraphrasing Hegel, Marx remarked that all the great
events and personages of world history occur, so to speak,
twice: the first time as tragedy, the second as farce.[64] It may
be true that Nazi-fascist imperialism was a parody – or, if it
is preferred, a ghost – of English nationalist imperialism; that
Soviet internationalism was a caricature of Napoleonic internationalism; and that the current *Pax Americana* parodies the
Pax Britannica. So far as the present analysis is concerned, it is
enough to have shown that a certain analogy can be established between the first three phases of English imperialism
distinguished in the last chapter, and the three phases which
imperialism has passed through during the last sixty years.
Once English world hegemony had declined for ever, imperialism again assumed successively a formal and informal national-

[64] K. Marx, 'The Eighteenth Brumaire of Louis Bonaparte', in *Surveys from
Exile*, Pelican/NLR, London 1973, p. 146.

Reaganites don't see that the
reassertion has *happened*,
nor why

ist cast. History would thereafter seem to have confirmed the
judgment implicit in Hobson's grid, according to which the
imperialism of the powers emerging at the end of the last century would issue, in the last analysis, into an 'internationalism'
(§13).

It remains to be seen whether the position I_3, currently
occupied by US imperialism, will somehow become 'stable', or
whether the reduplication of English imperialism will move
inexorably towards the conclusion I_4. The question may be
posed in a different way: is Hobson's concept of imperialism
(that is, precisely I_4) of purely historiographical interest, or
may it rather gain fresh topicality in the future?

In order to solve this problem, we must make quite clear the
limits of the analogical exercise which allowed us to discern a
reduplication of the English imperialism of bygone times in the
expansionist tendencies of the last sixty years. First, it is evident that the analogies are somewhat forced. It is as if we had
asked ourselves: given that imperialism has these four meanings, and these alone, which corresponds best to the characteristic tendencies of this or that epoch? Restricted in this way,
we were virtually compelled to make the choice we did and to
attach the same significance to ensembles of tendencies which
are, in many respects, extremely diverse. The purpose of the
undertaking was to show that when we speak today of imperialism, referring to the major processes of our epoch, we are
talking of something completely different from the object of
Hobson's discourse – and antithetical to that of Lenin.

However, by ascribing an identical significance to different
ensembles, the operation has inevitably cancelled the differences between them. Some of these have already been mentioned
in the course of the exposition – for example, the distinction
between the two colonial revolutions which closed the two
phases of nationalist imperialism (§14) or that between the
'content' (free trade or free enterprise) of the two phases of
informal imperialism (§16). It is almost as if our grid were
incapable of clarifying simultaneously the images of the first and
the second cycle of imperialism; and since we defined the grid
with reference to the characteristic tendencies of the first

cycle (that of English hegemony) the images which relate to the second emerge a little blurred.

In reality, Hobson's grid has certain very precise temporal limits. In order to grasp these, it suffices to point out that the grid, defined as the ensemble of expansionist tendencies of the nation-state, has no meaning before the rise of English world hegemony. Since its (analytical) origin lies in the nation-state (NS) it is in no position to represent either the imperialism of ancient Rome, for example, or even that of Holland in the first half of the 17th century: only with the English Navigation Acts did the nation-state become a dominant force on the world arena and only two hundred years later did it become the basic 'cell' of the international system.

The grid is at one and the same time the image and the 'product' of the historical process which structured the world in nation-states: it has no existence apart from the tendencies it seeks to represent. Hobson, who was active as a theoretician at the close of the first cycle of imperialism, could define the grid and thereby demonstrate the meaning of events at that historical moment; and it is only in relation to that precise point in time that the grid is in perfect 'focus'. Any attempt to project it backwards or forwards cannot but produce images which are to some extent blurred: before that point, the nation-state, which was the analytical origin of the representation, had not yet been fully constituted as the cell of the international system; while later, the cell itself underwent alterations which are reflected in the object of the representation.

These were complex mutations, investigation of which is beyond the scope of this essay. Their nature may, however, be surmised by comparing the 'imperial dualism' characteristic of the first cycle of imperialism with that which has marked the second cycle. In both instances, a given power (France in the first, the USSR in the second), unable to attain a position of absolute hegemony, attempted to oppose a more strictly political empire of a continental character to the universalistic tendency of the imperialism of the hegemonic power (England and the United States, respectively). But whereas in the former case France and England were true and proper nation-states, in the latter case, the USA and the USSR are nation-states with quite novel and specific features. The difference lies not only in their continental dimension, but also in the fact that the 'internalization' of territorial expansionism produced, on the one hand, a nation structured in a plurality of states, the *United States* of America, and on the other hand, a multinational state in the USSR. In both countries, the coincidence of state and nation, which lies at the origin of Hobson's grid, is much fainter than it was in France or England. What is the significance of this change, which has been intentionally disregarded in our schema of the reduplication of English imperialism? Could it not imply that the second cycle of imperialism converges at N^- instead of at S^+, or, worse still, that the whole representation based on the expansion of NS loses significance, that is, relevance?

The current crisis of the nation-state, which is manifested both in the tendency to multinational and/or multistate aggregations and in the parallel process of internal decomposition of nation-states into ethnically more or less homogeneous regional entities, does indeed tend to diminish the significance of the above representation, and thus of any attempt to predict future trends on the basis of it. But quite apart from this, it is necessary to keep in mind a third limit of Hobson's grid, such as we have so far represented it – namely, its two-dimensional character.

The circular and repetitive movement attributed to expansionist phenomena actually depends on the assumption of a two-dimensional space with which to represent them. If we confined ourselves to a single dimension, the movement would be linear in type (§6): $S^- \rightarrow S \rightarrow S^+$ could thus indicate the tendency of state expansionism to pass from a factor of order and peace into a factor of anarchy and war; and $N^+ \rightarrow N \rightarrow N^-$, the tendency of the expansionism of peoples and nations to change, according to Schumpeter's picture,[65] from an antagonistic phenomenon into a non-antagonistic one, at least at

---

[65] For Schumpeter, imperialism is an irrationalist residue from the past, which tends to disappear with the progressive rationalization of peoples' way

the level of political relations. Evidently, if we introduced a third dimension, the movement would no longer be either linear or circular, but would assume a form corresponding to the nature of this third dimension. Any judgment on the actual convergence of the tendencies will therefore have to await a three-dimensional redefinition of them. This is what we shall undertake in the next chapter.

---

of life and thinking: 'We must expect to see [the imperialist] impulse, which rests on the primitive contingencies of physical combat, gradually disappear, washed away by new exigencies of daily life . . . The competitive system absorbs the full energies of most of the people at all economic levels. Constant application, attention, and concentration of energy are the conditions of survival within it . . . There is much less excess energy to be vented in war and conquest than in any precapitalist society.' Op. cit., p. 69.

4.

The Dissolution

From Finance Capital to Multinational Enterprises

19. At this point, the reader may ask the reason for our delay in introducing that association between imperialism and *capitalism* which, after all, constitutes the kernel of Hobson's *Study*. In fact, we have so far been concerned to explain what was for Hobson so obvious that it could be passed over in silence or condensed into a few introductory pages and scattered remarks. But now that the conceptual grid within which Hobson reasoned has been explicated, we are in a position to summarize his economic analysis without serious risk of being misunderstood.

It should be noted at the outset that the representation of capitalism cannot be reduced to the space defined by the various forms of expansion of the nation-state. Capitalist phenomena have since their origin had a *supranational* character which cannot be designated by any of the arrows or arcs defined so far. These arrows and arcs can at the most denote phenomena of a *mercantile* nature which form part of, but by no means exhaust, the ensemble of capitalist processes.

There is, in fact, a substantive identity between the tendency towards a single world market and the rise of the nation-state to the position of a dominant reality of the international system. Thus, an eminent academic of the Bismarck era, Schmoller, could assert that mercantilism 'in its inmost kernel is nothing but state-making – not state-making in a narrow sense, but state-making and national-economy-making at the same time'.[66] More recently, Immanuel Wallerstein has argued that:

---

[66] Quoted in C. Wilson, *Mercantilism*, London 1958, p. 6.

Capital has never allowed its aspirations to be determined by national boundaries in a capitalist world-economy, and . . . the creation of 'national' barriers – generically, mercantilism – has historically been a defensive mechanism of capitalists located in states which are one level below the high point of strength in the system. Such was the case of England *vis-à-vis* the Netherlands in 1660–1715, France *vis-à-vis* Britain in 1715–1815, Germany *vis-à-vis* Britain in the nineteenth century, the Soviet Union *vis-à-vis* the US in the twentieth. In the process a large number of countries create national economic barriers whose consequences often last beyond their initial objectives. At this later point in the process the very same capitalists who pressed their national governments to impose the restrictions now find these restrictions constraining.[67]

It is obviously difficult to represent this vision in the terms defined by Hobson's grid. But if we bear in mind the association established above (§10) between nationalism and protectionism, it is possible to reinterpret the diagram of Fig. 8 in terms of tendencies towards the break-up and recomposition of the unity of the world market. Thus, the arcs $S^+ \rightarrow N^+, N^+ \rightarrow S^-, S^- \rightarrow N^-$, and $N^- \rightarrow S^+$ could represent the tendency of the hegemonic power to pass from one form to another of integration of the world market (or to vary the form according to the concrete situation); the arrows $N^+ \rightarrow NS$ and $S^- \rightarrow NS$, the tendencies generated in peripheral or semi-peripheral countries to separate off national markets for relative protection from foreign market competition; and lastly, the arrows $NS \rightarrow N^-$ and $NS \rightarrow S^+$ could represent the tendency of these countries to outgrow the dimensions of the national market, whether by openly accepting competition on the world market or by encompassing other peoples and nations within the protective barriers erected by the state.

Below (§22) we shall make more precise the possibility of such isomorphism between the plane defined by expansion of the nation-state and that defined by expansion of commodity-capital. For the moment, we will seek to show that for Hobson

---

[67] I. Wallerstein, 'The Rise and Future Demise of the World Capitalist System: Concepts for Comparative Analysis', *Comparative Studies in Society and History*, XVI, 4, September 1974, p. 402.

the dimension 'capitalism' is not reducible to the level of market relations, nor even to the plane defined by expansion of the nation-state. For this purpose, it will suffice to examine briefly his *explicit* theory of imperialism, that is to say, the nature of the tendencies to which he attributed the transformation of England from a free-trade power to an imperialist power *tout court*.

Hobson ruled out from the start the possibility that such a transformation corresponded to the interests of the nation *as a whole*:

> A completely socialist State which kept good books and presented regular balance-sheets of expenditure and assets would soon discard Imperialism; an intelligent *laissez-faire* democracy which gave duly proportionate weight in its policy to all economic interests alike would do the same.[68]

Of course, the fact that imperialism was a bad business for the nation did not mean that it could not be very good business for certain groups within it. Among these groups Hobson mentions in the first place the producers of armaments and means of maritime transport, shipping companies and other rather uncompetitive sectors of export industry.[69]

Dealing next with the necessarily protectionist effects of imperialism, Hobson also speaks of the support which such a policy could obtain from all those productive sectors that felt threatened by growing foreign competition.[70] These sectors, however, were not actively imperialist and, with the aim of strengthening their medium-term competitiveness, they could well have supported a policy of intensive development of the nation, of the kind envisaged by Hobson (cf. §12).

It would seem then that, in Hobson's view of things, the general interest of the nation indubitably lay with free trade; but that particular interests, endowed with higher 'specific weight' because of the greater concentration and cohesion of

[68] Hobson, op. cit., p. 47.
[69] Ibid., pp. 47–50.
[70] Ibid., pp. 102–5.

the groups which were their bearers, could thwart a choice
between free trade and imperialism. The resultant political
indeterminacy corresponds to the indeterminacy of Hobson's
judgment on the nature of nationalism (§6); and it may thus also
be designated by the divarication of $NS \rightarrow N^-$ and $NS \rightarrow S^+$ –
that is, the circumstance that the *internal* economic forces of
the nation-state generate divergent tendencies: one towards
free trade, the other towards imperialism. It is true that the
worsening of the competitive position of such forces on the
world market would tend to draw the compass-needle towards
S^+. Yet such a deterioration was not an inevitable fact: it
depended upon which of the two paths had been entered by the
nation-state. If it set out to develop intensively the resources
of the nation, the competitive sectors of the economy – and with
them the free-trade tendencies – would be strengthened as a
result; but if it took the course of squandering resources by
competing with other states in territorial expansion and
armaments, then the competitiveness of the national economy
would decline and the tendency to imperialism increase.

But which of the forces internal to the nation corresponds to
the arc $N^- \rightarrow S^+$, which in previous representations determined
the convergence of the system at S^+? The answer would seem to
be: that heterogeneous ensemble of forces which Hobson
defined as 'imperialist by conviction and by professional
interest',[71] in other words those sectors of the unproductive
middle classes for whom the new imperialism opened up broad
and prestigious vistas – professional soldiers, explorers, adven-
turers, missionaries, colonial administrators, and in general
all those who had a material as well as ideal interest in the world
hegemony of their own mother-country. For Hobson, however,
these forces provided only 'the motor-power' of imperialism.
Left to themselves, they were in no position to impress a clear
direction on state policy: 'The enthusiasm for expansion which
issues from these sources, though strong and genuine, is irregu-
lar and blind.' The 'imperial engine' needed a governor to direct
its operation.[72]

[71] Ibid., p. 50.
[72] Ibid., p. 59.

20. For Hobson, then, it was not the economic and social forces considered so far which determined the direction of contemporary change. It was rather an ensemble of forces which he variously designated by the terms: finance, money-lending classes, financial plutocracy, and so on, and which we shall term, according to current usage, *finance capital* or *finance capitalism.*

In defining this ensemble of forces Hobson, even before he mentions his well-known theory of underconsumption, speaks of another tendency which some of his rather careless critics, such as Emmanuel, have accused him of ignoring:[73]

> It appears that the period of energetic Imperialism coincided with a remarkable growth in the income for foreign investment.... To a larger extent every year Great Britain has been becoming a nation living upon tribute from abroad, and classes who enjoy this tribute have had an ever-increasing incentive to employ the public policy, the public purse, and the public force to extend the field of their private investments, and to safeguard and improve their existing investments.[74]

This group of 'investors', who absorbed the rising flow of dividends and interest on funds invested abroad, constitute the first component of Hobson's concept of Finance Capital. However, as was the case with the economic and social forces just examined, such investors lacked the concentration and unity of purpose necessary to impose a direction on imperialist trends. Both politically and economically, they in general formed only 'the cat's-paws of the great financial houses, who use stocks and shares not so much as investments to yield them interest, but as material for speculation in the money market'.[75]

These great finance houses, which we shall term *high finance*, represent the second component of finance capital, to which Hobson attributed the role of 'governor of the imperial engine'. They had all the qualities required to manipulate the political life of nations:

[73] A. Emmanuel, op. cit.
[74] Hobson, op. cit., pp. 52–4.
[75] Ibid., p. 56.

These great businesses – banking, broking, bill-discounting, loan-floating, company-promoting – form the central ganglion of international capitalism. United by the strongest bonds of organisation, always in closest and quickest touch with one another, situated in the very heart of the business capital of every State, controlled, so far as Europe is concerned, chiefly by men of a single and peculiar race, who have behind them many centuries of financial experience, they are in a unique position to manipulate the policy of nations. . . . These men, holding their realised wealth and their business capital, as they must, chiefly in stocks and bonds, have a double stake, first as investors, but secondly and chiefly as financial dealers. *As investors, their political influence does not differ essentially from that of the smaller investors, except that they usually possess a practical control of the businesses in which they invest. As speculators or financial dealers they constitute, however, the gravest single factor in the economics of Imperialism.* To create new public debts, to float new companies and cause constant considerable fluctuations of values are three conditions of their profitable business. Each condition carries them into politics and throws them on the side of imperialism.[76]

In Hobson's view, then, high finance presents two main characteristics. In the first place, it is a *supranational* entity lying outside the plane defined by the expansion of the nation-state. Secondly, while not belonging to this plane, it nevertheless influences it in a critical manner. *For in so far as it is a speculative intermediary on the monetary market*, high finance tends to transform the excess liquidity present on the market into demand for new investment opportunities, that is, principally for state loans and territorial expansion.

A diagrammatic representation may assist an understanding of Hobson's concept of finance capital. In Fig. 12, this concept is designated by the ensemble $N^- \rightarrow F$, $F \rightarrow S^+$ and $NS \rightarrow F$, linking the plane defined by the expansion of NS to the point F (finance capital). The first two arrows of this ensemble correspond to the two components of finance capital which we have already defined. $N^- \rightarrow F$ designates the tendency of excess liquidity formation, resulting from the inflow of profits and dividends on money-capital invested abroad. Its origin at N^-

[76] Ibid., pp. 56–7. Emphasis added.

signifies that the tendency in question was based upon the
hegemonic position occupied by England within the informal
empire of free trade, while its 'divergence' from the plane
defined by the expansion of the nation-state signifies that it
nurtured, both economically and politically, the supranational
entity of high finance. The arrow $F \to S^+$ designates precisely
the characteristic tendency of this second component of finance
capital – that is, the tendency of high finance to press for territorial expansion by the state as a way of opening up new areas
of financial intermediation and speculation, whether through
investment of money-capital outside the national boundaries,
or through financing of the public debt of the expansionist
nation-state.

Fig. 12

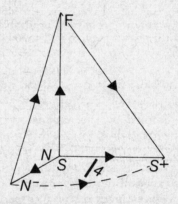

Before we consider the third component of finance capital
(that designated by NS $\to$ F in Fig. 12) we should underline the
significance which the arc $N^- \to S^+$ comes to assume in this
new representation. In the analysis developed in previous
chapters, this arc designated the policy of the hegemonic
power, which played a determining role in the convergence of
the international system at S^+. In the analysis developed in the
last section, however, it designated those social forces, 'imperialist by conviction and by profession', to which Hobson did
not attribute a determining role in shifting the internal
equilibria of the nation-state in the direction of an imperialist
policy, in the strict sense of the term. That is why, in Fig. 12, the

arc in question has been represented by means of a broken, rather than continuous, line. It thereby indicates the fact that, in Hobson's conception, English world hegemony did no more than reflect the domination of finance capital over mercantile capital – or money-capital over commodity-capital; that, in other words, the direction assumed by the imperialist social forces of the nation was simply a reflection of the tendencies proper to finance capital; and, in the final instance, that $N^- \to S^+$ was a reflection, on the plane defined by the expansion of NS, of the trajectory $N^- \to F \to S^+$.

Figure 12 also brings out the 'centrality' of the third component of finance capital (considered as an ensemble of tendencies dominating the plane defined by the expansion of NS, although not belonging to it) – the component designated by $NS \to F$. It seems to me that $NS \to F$ should designate that tendency to underconsumption, overproduction or excess savings (terms used interchangeably by Hobson) which he takes to be the 'tap-root' of imperialism.

Hobson defined this tendency with the help of concepts that were to become commonplace forty years later:

> All saving for investment does not imply slackness of production; quite the contrary. Saving is economically justified, from the social standpoint, when the capital in which it takes material shape finds full employment in helping to produce commodities which, when produced, will be consumed. It is saving in excess of this amount that causes mischief, taking shape in surplus capital which is not needed to assist current consumption, and which either lies idle, or tries to oust existing capital from its employment, or else seeks speculative use abroad under the protection of the Government.[77]

Thus, the excess liquidity which provided the economic and political sustenance of high finance did not originate solely, or even principally, in the inflow of interest and dividends on money-capital invested abroad. Of much greater importance was the very manner in which wealth was produced and distributed *within* the nation:

[77] Ibid., p. 82.

If a tendency to distribute income or consuming power according to needs were operative, it is evident that consumption would rise with every rise of producing power, for human needs are illimitable, and there could be no excess of saving. But it is quite otherwise in a state of economic society where distribution has no fixed relation to needs, but is determined by other conditions which assign to some people a consuming power vastly in excess of needs or possible uses, while others are destitute of consuming power enough to satisfy even the full demands of physical efficiency.[78]

The character of these 'other conditions' is straightaway clarified when Hobson, quoting *The Significance of the Trust* by H. G. Wilshire, explains the inelasticity of consumption relative to the social product by reference to the fact that competition among labourers tends to keep wages tied to the cost of living, preventing them from rising at the same rate as productivity. From this he concludes:

It is not industrial progress that demands the opening up of new markets and areas of investment, but mal-distribution of consuming power which prevents the absorption of commodities and capital within the country. The over-saving which is the economic root of Imperialism is found by analysis to consist of rents, monopoly profits, and other excessive elements of income, which, not being earned by labour of head or hand, have no legitimate *raison d'être*. . . . They form a surplus wealth, which, having no proper place in the normal economy of production and consumption, tends to accumulate as excessive savings. Let any turn in the tide of politico-economic forces divert from these owners their excess of income and make it flow, either to the workers in higher wages, or to the community in taxes, so that it will be spent instead of being saved, serving in either of these ways to swell the tide of consumption – there will be no need to fight for foreign markets or foreign areas of investment.[79]

For Hobson, then, a reversal of the tendency to underconsumption would be enough to restrain any trend for England to become transformed from a free-trade power into an imperialist one *tout court*. In the terms of the diagram of Fig. 12, the direc-

[78] Ibid., p. 83.
[79] Ibid., pp. 85–6.

tion of the arrow NS → F would have only to be reversed to weaken the 'circuit' $N^- \to F \to S^+$, of which $N^- \to S^+$ is simply a reflection on the plane defined by the expansion of the nation-state. As we shall see in a moment, it was not long before such a reversal was accomplished in reality – not at the tempo or in the mode envisaged by Hobson, but through just those events that he sought to avoid.

21. Our task is now to show how, in the first half of this century, the thirty-year period of world-wide anarchy and war produced an irreversible mutation in that ensemble of tendencies with reference to which Hobson defined the imperialism of his epoch. But we should first extend the three-dimensional representation beyond the quadrant I_4 (to which we temporarily limited it) to cover the whole plane defined by the expansion of the nation-state. With this purpose in mind, we shall take as our starting-point an image of high finance which is in certain respects identical, and in others opposite, to that of Hobson.

I am referring to Polanyi's authoritative account which stresses, like Hobson's *Study*, the supranational character of high finance, but at the same time defines it as the principal factor of peace operating among the great powers in the second half of the 19th century:

> The Concert of Europe, which succeeded [the Holy Alliance] lacked the feudal as well as the clerical tentacles. . . . And yet what the Holy Alliance, with its complete unity of thought and purpose, could achieve in Europe only with the help of frequent armed interventions was here accomplished on a world scale by the shadowy entity called the Concert of Europe with the help of a very much less frequent and oppressive use of force. For an explanation of this amazing feat, we must seek for some undisclosed powerful social instrumentality at work in the new setting, which could play the role of dynasties and episcopacies under the old and make the peace interest effective. This anonymous factor was *haute finance*. . . .
>
> Both the personnel and the motives of this singular body invested it with a status the roots of which were securely grounded in the private sphere of strictly business interest. The Rothschilds were subject to no one government; as a family they embodied the

abstract principle of internationalism; their loyalty was to a firm, the credit of which had become the only supranational link between political government and industrial effort in a swiftly growing world economy. In the last resort, their independence sprang from the needs of the time which demanded a sovereign agent commanding the confidence of national statesmen and of the international investors alike; it was to this vital need that the metaphysical extraterritoriality of a Jewish bankers' dynasty domiciled in the capitals of Europe provided an almost perfect solution. They were anything but pacifist; they had made their fortune in the financing of wars; they were impervious to moral consideration; they had no objection to any number of minor, short, or localized wars. But their business would be impaired if a general war between the Great Powers should interfere with the monetary foundations of the system. By the logic of fact it fell to them to maintain the requisites of general peace in the midst of the revolutionary transformation to which the peoples of the planet were subject.[80]

Although this assessment of high finance is diametrically opposed to that of Hobson, their incompatibility is less radical than it may appear at first sight. Hobson himself acknowledged that the policies of high finance did not, in each and every situation, point in the direction of war, and even that 'where war would bring about too great and too permanent a damage to the substantial fabric of industry, which is the ultimate and essential basis of speculation, their influence is cast for peace'.[81] Polanyi, for his part, acknowledged that high finance was compelled by the nature of its activities 'to tie itself to those governments whose objective was power and conquest'[82] – an objective which inevitably aroused rivalry among states.

In reality, the contradiction between these two points of view reflected an effective contradiction within high finance itself. As an embodiment of money-capital, high finance had no specific competitive position of its own, and it thus depended on expansion of the political power of one or more states beyond their national boundaries – both in order to protect its past investments and to create new opportunities for financial

[80] Polanyi, op. cit., pp. 9–11.
[81] Hobson, op. cit., p. 58.
[82] Polanyi, op. cit., p. 11.

intermediation and speculation. At the same time, however, it had to try to prevent the inter-state rivalry fuelled by such expansion from resulting in a world war and therewith in the evaporation of its own patrimonial assets.

In Fig. 13, which extends the dimension 'finance capital' to the whole plane defined by the expansion of the nation-state, we designate by means of the two arrows $F \to S^+$ and $F \to S^-$ this tendency of high finance to promote expansion of the political power of one or more states beyond their national boundaries. Compared with the representation of Fig. 12, this has the advantage of demonstrating how the tendencies activated by high finance produce an effect of war or peace, according to the international situation in which they are inserted. Thus, in the circumstances prevailing in the early 19th century, the tendency of high finance to sustain English formal imperialism contributed to the realization of a hierarchical order among states serving to foster universal peace ($F \to S^-$); in the context marking the end of the century, the same tendency came to assume an altogether opposite significance ($F \to S^+$) – namely, that of a tendency towards universal war.

Fig. 13

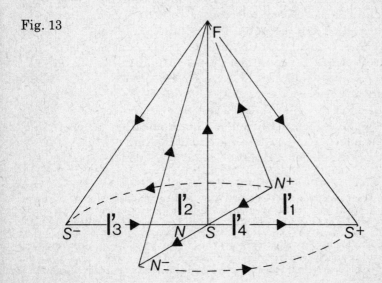

Figure 13 further shows that high finance may not only activate tendencies of opposite significance, but also itself be furthered by tendencies (N^- → F and N^+ → F) whose matrices are of opposite significance. We saw in the last section how N^- → F designates the tendency of high finance to be sustained from the influx of interest and dividends on money-capital which English investors had placed abroad. The very existence of this flow evidently depended upon the achievement of a wide sphere of freedom for the international circulation of money, goods and capital; indeed, that is why we have designated the tendency in question by means of an arrow 'originating' at N^-. The arrow N^+ → F which is now introduced designates instead the tendency of high finance to be sustained by money flows, just as 'parasitic' as those mentioned above, but with an opposite mercantile basis – that is, profits 'originating' in the *monopolistic* control exercised by the colonialist nation-state over the territory and resources of the colonies.[83]

The limited aims of the present investigation do not allow us to specify by means of a synchronic-diachronic analysis similar to that developed in previous chapters, the significance of these tendencies and of their various combinations in three-dimensional space. For our purposes, two brief specifications will suffice. It should be noted first of all that, despite Hobson's hypothesis, not all transmutations of hegemony may be defined as 'reflections' of tendencies proper to finance capital: only the two arcs drawn in Fig. 13 (i.e., N^+ → S^- and N^- → S^+) can be defined in this way – the first as a reflection of N^+ → F → S^-, the second of N^- → F → S^+. These two arcs correspond to those we employed in order to define synchronically the imperialism of the hegemonic power at the end of the 19th century – that is, the specific object of Hobson's study (§7) – which may therefore

---

[83] The connection between monopoly and colonialism was the kernel of mercantilist theory and practice. As Dobb has pointed out (*Studies in the Development of Capitalism*, London 1963, p. 204), this policy 'chiefly depended for its success on its application to a system of colonial trade, where political influence could be brought to bear to ensure to the parent country some element of monopoly; and it is essentially as applied to the exploitation of a dependent colonial system that mercantilist trade-theories acquired a meaning'.

be comprehensively designated by the expression 'finance imperialism'. Such a definition cannot, however, be given of the two arcs $S^+ \rightarrow N^+$ and $S^- \rightarrow N^-$, the specific tendencies of nationalist imperialism and informal imperialism.

We shall see shortly that this impossibility can be validated at the historico-empirical level and that, nevertheless, it does not prevent us from defining the whole course of English imperialism within the system represented in Fig. 13. But it is first necessary to proceed to a second specification. What, we must ask ourselves, is the significance in a diachronic analysis of the fact that the three-dimensional spaces of Fig. 13 (I'_1, I'_2, I'_3 and I'_4) have the arrow NS $\rightarrow$ F in common? It naturally does not mean that the two-and-a-half centuries between the passing of the Navigation Acts and the outbreak of the First World War were *uniformly* characterized by a tendency to underconsumption (which is the precise meaning we attached to NS $\rightarrow$ F in section 20). It rather signifies that, *beyond cyclical fluctuations and short-to-medium-term countertendencies*, it was in just this period that an alternation of mechanisms, now compulsory (political) now spontaneous (economic), transformed the bases of production and consumption within the hegemonic nation-state in the direction of capitalism. Whereas in the England of the first half of the 17th century the vast majority of income from labour was tied to the progress of productivity, in the two-and-a-half centuries that followed, a growing proportion of such income did not advance in step with a sharply rising productivity, but tended to be equated with 'the cost of living' – or, to be more precise, with the reproduction costs of labour-power.

According to Hobson's hypothesis, this tendency of itself possessed strong underconsumptionist implications (§20), which were then intensified by another long-term trend – that of the state to pass from a generally inflationary policy, typical of the late middle ages and the first century of the modern era, to a generally deflationary policy.[84] These considerations sug-

---

[84] Mercantilist policies were also, in my opinion, *ultimately* deflationist, because of the crucial role they attached to state thesaurization of precious metals.

gest the hypothesis that the tendency to underconsumption defined by Hobson, while only revealing itself over considerable periods of time, may in a certain sense be regarded not only as the 'tap-root' of late 18th century English imperialism, but also as the underlying trend of its two-and-a-half centuries of historical development.

However, the 'limit' of this tendency lay precisely in the system of tendencies of which it was the specific and principal feature. In fact, the system represented in Fig. 13 has its point of convergence at S^+ in a state of universal anarchy and war.[85] Now, leaving aside the destructive effects of such a state on the international monetary system, war is the most effective counter-tendency to underconsumption known in history. The actual attainment of position S^+ therefore signifies the reversal of the direction of NS $\rightarrow$ F and, thus a progressive 'dissolution' of the whole system represented in Fig. 13.

As we shall see in the next section, such a scenario is essentially what occurred in the period encompassing the Two World Wars – and in such a manner that the end of English imperialism coincided with the end of the domination of money-capital over commodity-capital. The reversal of NS $\rightarrow$ F, envisaged by Hobson as the antidote to imperialism (§20), was thereby realized with a quite different tempo and modality: Hobson expected the reversal to be achieved in time to avert convergence at S^+, and in such a way that the circuit $N^- \rightarrow F \rightarrow S^+$ would be weakened and the circuit $N^- \rightarrow F \rightarrow$ NS $\rightarrow N^-$ unleashed; in reality, the reversal took place precisely by passing through convergence at S^+.

22. The nationalist imperialism of the first half of this century

[85] We could of course consider the transition from one form of hegemony to another as autonomous tendencies, rather than as reflections of tendencies proper to finance capital. But we should then have to trace the unbroken arcs $S^+ \rightarrow N^+$, $N \rightarrow S^-$, $S^- \rightarrow N^-$ and $N^- \rightarrow S^+$ even in the three-dimensional representation. In that way, an element of overdetermination would be introduced into the system of tendencies represented in Fig. 13, and convergence at S^+ would become relative rather than absolute. The argument would thus become more complex without changing anything of substance in the conclusions.

can no longer be understood in the terms defined by the ensemble of tendencies represented by Fig. 13, which we shall
henceforth term 'finance imperialism'. Militarism and war
gave an extraordinary impetus to self-financing of industrial
firms and to public expenditure – a process which spelt the
definitive eclipse of the domination of money-capital over
commodity-capital.

> The victory of internal financing over the borrowing from banks,
> savings banks, and insurance institutions indicates the decline of
> the role of banking capital. That decline is a universal trend and is
> as operative in the United States as it is in Germany. This trend
> seems to be determined by the decline in the pace of economic
> expansion; by the monopolistic and cartel structure, which, by
> granting differential rents, facilitates the internal accumulation of
> capital; by the growth of institutional investments, government
> spending and financing.[86]

German imperialism, which dominated the period encompassing the two world wars, neither initially possessed nor
ultimately acquired a supranational capitalist dimension: it
functioned entirely on the plane defined by the expansion of
the nation-state, which, as will be recalled (§19), may also
designate the various expansionist tendencies of the national
market.

Japanese, too

> Since the world market is divided among powerful contending
> states, it can no longer be conquered by trade and investment but
> only by political means. And since trade between industrial states
> is the essence of foreign trade, the political conquest of the world is
> and must be the aim of National Socialist Germany if she wants to
> survive as a highly industrialized nation. . . . It is the high pro-
> ductivity of the industrial apparatus, the pressure for foreign
> markets, and the need for satisfying the vital material interests of
> her masses that have driven Germany into a policy of conquest and
> will continue to drive her to still further expansion until she is
> defeated or has fulfilled her aim. It is the dynamics of a fairly young,
> aggressive, monopolized country that is the prime mover of Ger-
> many's expansion.[87]

[86] F. Neumann, *Behemoth*, London 1942, pp. 261–2.
[87] Ibid., pp. 275–6.

German nationalist imperialism, in other words, could in no way be defined as a 'reflection' of tendencies mediated by a supranational entity, such as high finance. It must rather be represented as the ensemble of tendencies autonomously generated on the plane of relations between nation-states and commodity-capitals. Thus, the representation given in sections 13 and 14 has need of no further elaboration, except for a re-definition of its various component images in terms of the expansion of commodity-capitals rather than nation-states. In particular, it is necessary to reconsider the image of 'living space', which somewhat mysteriously always recurred among the principal motivations of nationalist imperialism. The passage from Neumann just quoted suggests that something was indeed concealed behind this image: not so much the abstract goal of territory to ensure the nation's survival, but the concrete need for new sources and outlets of production experienced by a sharply expanding national industry – one which, as a late-comer, found itself constricted by the narrow boundaries of the nation-state and the already existing interests of the other national markets.

From this point of view, German nationalist imperialism did not differ substantively from that which developed in England two-and-a-half centuries earlier. Then, too, the expansionism of the young English nation could in no way be defined as a reflection of tendencies inherent in a supranational entity. Indeed, the great commercial firms, which were in certain respects the progenitors of high finance, seem to have opposed, rather than promoted, the development of English nationalism in an imperialist direction:

The Navigation Act of 1651 represented the victory of a *national* trading interest over the separate interests and privileges of the companies. It was naturally disliked by some members of the old companies, though the Levant and Eastland Companies favoured it. It contributed to the victory of the English New Draperies over their Dutch rivals. The navigation system also benefited England's artisans by protecting the home market from Dutch competition and by increasing colonial and overseas markets, at the same time that any colonial industrial development which would compete with England's was prohibited.[88]

The difference between the two cases[89] consists in the fact that English imperialism succeeded in converting its own political hegemony into a financial supremacy tending to become supranational: the century of world-wide anarchy and war that followed the Navigation Acts not only gave England domination of the seas, but also made it the centre of international finance, thereby creating the premises of the later phases of formal and informal imperialism. In the terms of our three-dimensional grid, this path may be designated, as in Fig. 11, by means of an arc $NS \to N^+$ (§14) – but with the difference that the arc now 'releases' not only the arrow $N^+ \to NS$, but also the arrow $N^+ \to F$, which in its turn issues in the tendency designated by $F \to S^-$ (as indicated in Fig. 14).[90]

Owing to the different historical situation in which it emerged, the nationalist imperialism of Germany did not release any tendency to supranationality from its own capitalist dimension. Far from evolving in a supranational direction, German finance capitalism was subordinated to, and subsumed under, the nation-state and industrial capital. In other words, National-Socialist imperialism remained anchored in the plane defined by the expansion of the nation-state (and of commodity-capital), and its trajectory can still be designated, as in the two-dimensional representation of Fig. 11, by means of a circle inscribed in the quadrant I_1 (cf. §14).

[88] C. Hill, *Reformation to Industrial Revolution*, London 1967, p. 125. Emphasis in the original.

[89] I am, of course, referring exclusively to our conceptual grid: from other points of view the differences are still more striking.

[90] It follows that, besides $N^- \to S^+$, the characteristic transformation of formal imperialism ($N^+ \to S^-$) may also be conceived as a reflection of tendencies proper to finance capital. That is why the arc that designates it in Fig. 14 has been represented as a *broken* line. By contrast, the characteristic transformations of the nationalist and informal phases of English imperialism ($NS \to N^+$ and $S^- \to N^-$) cannot be pictured in the same way. They 'release', but are not determined by, tendencies peculiar to finance capital. Indeed, the latter would in themselves imply transformations with opposite values ($N^+ \to S^+$ and $N^- \to S^-$). Thus, in Fig. 14, the arcs which designate them have

Fig. 14

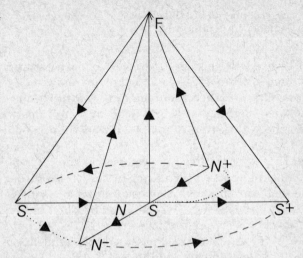

The outbreak of the First World War signalled the first fundamental break with the system of tendencies within which Hobson had defined the imperialism of the close of the 19th century. Lenin's perception of this break represents his second great insight. (The first, it will be recalled, was his realization that the nationalism of the colonial areas defined, at the level of international relations, the limits of the imperialism of his epoch.) In fact, Lenin, like Hobson, put the concept of 'finance capital' at the centre of his analysis of imperialism; he differed from Hobson in stressing its mercantilist aspects and, above all, its tendency to pass into 'state capitalism'.

However, Lenin did not concern himself with the fact that the newly-emerging powers were bearers of diverse models of expansionism, and that consequently shifts in the relationship of forces between nation-states – correlated to phenomena of uneven development – would not necessarily strengthen the model of imperialism which he analysed. This is what we shall

_____

been *dotted*, precisely in order to indicate that they refer to historical trajectories, whose determination has to be sought at various levels of the financial-economic order – for example, at the political-mercantile level to which I am now referring in the text.

now attempt to demonstrate by developing the analysis of American imperialism sketched in the last chapter.

23. In analysing the association between imperialism and American capitalism, we should first note that, as in the German case, the domination of finance capital over industrial capital proved to be an altogether transient phenomenon. As Sweezy has pointed out with specific reference to the USA:

> With . . . internal sources of additional capital at their disposal, corporate managements are to a greater or less degree freed from dependence on the market for new securities as a source of capital, and by the same token they are freed from their dependence on bankers. To be sure, where the influence of banks is firmly entrenched this does not mean an immediate decline in their power. But in the long run, economic power which is related to no economic function is bound to weaken and eventually disappear. This is exactly what happens to the power of the banks in so far as it is based on control over the issuance of new securities. The function itself atrophies and the power to which it gave rise declines, leaving the banks in a secondary position.[91]

From the point of view that directly interests us, more recent historiography has since demonstrated that, even in its golden age, US high finance did not dominate American foreign policy as much as has generally been thought: 'except in Asia . . . the industrial corporation was the key element in the political economy of American foreign policy after 1895 – and even there the Open Door Policy was ultimately interpreted from their point of view'.[92] In any case, the inter-war period witnessed the definitive subordination of finance capital to industrial capital in the process of their expansion:

[91] Sweezy, op. cit. (1946), pp. 267–8. Sweezy has recently reaffirmed this position in a polemic with a series of articles by Fitch and Oppenheimer published by the review *Socialist Revolution*. His reply seems to me quite exhaustive. But just for that reason, I cannot agree with the conclusion that present-day multinationals correspond perfectly to Lenin's concept of 'finance capital'. ('The Resurgence of Financial Control: Fact or Fancy?' *Monthly Review*, XXIII, 6, November 1971, esp. p. 31).

[92] W. A. Williams, 'The Large Corporation and American Foreign Policy' in D. Horowitz (ed.) *Corporations and the Cold War*, New York and London 1969, p. 84.

The bankers naturally stressed operations which would provide them with a steady return on investment. Ideally, and for that reason, they favoured direct ties with foreign governments in preference to subordinate collaboration with industrial corporations. Until the Great Depression therefore, they seldom cooperated directly in the program of overseas industrial expansion. But the crash forced them to accept such an approach, and after the mid-1930s they worked ever more closely with the industrialists, and with the government which pushed an industrial policy.[93]

In those same years, the launching of Roosevelt's New Deal seemed to detonate in America that tendency to state capitalism which we have seen to be the specific characteristic of German imperialism. Even if this tendency did not go so far as it had done in Germany, it served as the prelude to changes in economic policy which, after the Second World War, would render the decline of finance capital as a supranational economic entity dominating inter-state relations irreversible. I am referring to the so-called Keynesian revolution which, as it concerns us here, essentially consisted in the institutionalization in peacetime conditions of certain characteristic policies of a war economy, such as deficit spending and state control of liquidity, whether directly or through the central banks. It is well known that these practices effectively prevented the reappearance of major tendencies towards underconsumption or systematic formation of excess liquidity, which had traditionally fuelled finance capital in time of peace. Thus, the supersession under US hegemony of the state of universal anarchy and war did not reactivate the domination of finance capital, but consolidated the reversal of the tendency to underconsumption, and with it the progressive 'dissolution' of the entire system represented in Fig. 13. If, from this point of view, US imperialism completed and consolidated the work of German imperialism, in other respects it clearly distanced itself from the latter. The differences between the two were in effect, much more important than their similarities. American, unlike German, imperialism was evolving in a supranational direction even before the USA succeeded in asserting its world hegemony.

[93] Ibid., p. 82.

post-'45 expansion novel —
not mercantile, not finance-
capital

The Dissolution   133

More precisely, the rise of US hegemony and the acquisition by US capitalism of a supranational dimension were co-extensive phenomena, virtually two sides of the same coin.

This supranational dimension may appear at first sight as a simple external projection of large national firms, which had already acquired continental dimensions within the USA:

> US corporations began to move to foreign countries almost as soon as they had completed their continent-wide integration. . . . In becoming national firms, US corporations learned how to become international. Also, their large size and oligopolistic position gave them an incentive. Direct investment became a new weapon in their arsenal of oligopolistic rivalry. Instead of joining a cartel (prohibited under US law), they invested in foreign customers, suppliers, and competitors.[94]

We shall see shortly that this expansion must be sharply distinguished both from mercantile (export/import of commodity-capital) and from financial (export/import of money-capital) expansion, and that it represents an altogether novel phenomenon. For the moment, let us simply note that it was initially propelled by the spreading of those protectionist barriers which, about the end of the century, were more and more hampering the international movement of commodity-capital, and which, after the outbreak of the First World War, dealt a sharp blow to exporters of money-capital. The reasons for this are quite evident. Direct investment was often the only way for the large firm to circumvent, or rather transform into a competitive advantage, those obstacles which had been gradually erected in the path of its expansion through import and export of commodity-capital. The war subsequently accelerated the tendency in question, giving a fresh impetus to concentration of capital, developing transport and international communications technology, financially strengthening the United States in relation to the traditional centres of money-capital accumulation (§12) and, within the country itself, reinforcing the large

---

[94] S. Hymer, 'The Multinational Corporation and the Law of Uneven Development' in J. N. Bhagwati (ed.) *Economics and World Order*, World Law Fund, New York 1970.

corporation *vis-à-vis* high finance.

At the turn of the century and above all during the First World War, there were thus two main waves of 'emigration' of US big industry: towards Europe and towards Latin America. In the 1930's, however, concomitantly with the complete breakdown of the unity of the world market, the phenomenon registered a certain ebb, which indicated that it had reached the limits of its possibility in a world dominated by nationalism. The nature of these limits may easily be discerned from a brief examination of the genesis of the multinational firm in the first half of this century.

In the first stages of a firm's multinational expansion, when, for example, it is concerned simply to capture a new national market by establishing a plant there, direct investment is attracted by state protection of that market – provided, of course, that the latter is of sufficient size to allow the employment of the techniques of production and distribution which secure the competitive advantage of the expanding firm. After that stage has been reached, however, the protected markets may become too narrow, whether because the overseas subsidiary's production has reached the limits of 'simple expansion', or because the parent company's techniques of production or distribution, or both, have evolved in such a way that they need a larger scale of production.

At this point, it becomes necessary to export to other national economies the commodities or, still better, the profits which have been produced by the subsidiary. In fact, any attempt to organize production on a multinational scale is pointless unless it is possible, without incurring excessive risks on the exchange, to convert the profits of the various subsidiaries into a means of payment that is universally accepted (or, at the very least, accepted in the country of the parent-company), and to repatriate them or transfer them from one country to another. This limit becomes 'absolute' when the multinational expansion of the firm does not have a purely 'extensive' character (multiplication of branches with a similar structure) but acquires an 'intensive' character, creating a more or less advanced division of labour between the parent-company and the subsidiaries themselves. In this third phase, international movements of commodities and money are nothing other than movements *internal* to the multinational company (and essential to its reproduction).

In the 1930's, few large American firms had entered this third phase of multinationalization, but many were already emerging from the first. In those same years, however, the tendency to disintegration of the world market was aggravated as a result of the collapse of the gold-standard and the international generalization of currency inconvertibility (§12). Thus, at the very moment when multinationalization of American big industry was beginning to make necessary a certain liberalization of international movements of commodity-capital and money-capital, the precondition of the former (i.e. convertibility of currencies) was actually lapsing.

A further obstacle was represented by the other characteristic tendency of modern nationalist imperialism – that is, the tendency of the capitalism of certain newly-emerging powers to be transformed into state capitalism (§22). In Russia the national economy was subtracted from the orbit of capitalism altogether by the October Revolution. The general process gradually spread, albeit in less radical forms and on diverse social bases, not only in Germany, but in some degree throughout Europe. The obstacles which state capitalism placed in the way of multinational expansion of the large American company were even more rigid than those connected with the growing restrictions on the international movement of commodity-capital and money-capital. But even without the explicitly hostile behaviour which at times marked the nationalism of certain European countries, the development of the big multinational companies encountered serious problems. In general, centralized state co-ordination of the different productive sectors of each national economy was strengthening structural interdependence within the nation-state and its colonial appendages, reducing or quite simply eliminating the field of penetration by foreign companies.

The Second World War sharpened this contradiction by aggravating the tendencies towards autarchy and state capi-

imp. for Ferguson argument

talism. At the same time, however, it ripened the conditions for a new wave of 'emigration' by US big industry, which in the space of twenty years would transform it into multinational capital proper. The impulses leading to multinationalization were similar to those of the epoch of the First World War. But they were of far greater intensity and scope: virtually all the world's gold reserves were concentrated in the United States; finance capital was all but incorporated into the large multi-branch firms; concentration of capital, and, even more, technology developed in such a way that even the vast territory of the North American nation became too narrow, and new outlets had to be sought in a unified world economy.

This was the politico-economic context that was formative for Roosevelt's vision, of which we spoke in the last chapter (§15). Without a political mediation – without, that is to say, formalization of US economic and military supremacy in a hierarchical inter-state order, serving to guarantee world peace – it would have been extremely difficult to create the conditions for such a rapid and relatively painless internationalization of US capital. As we know, this hierarchical order led, within little more than a decade, to the restoration of international currency convertibility, to the *de facto* overcoming of state capitalism in Western Europe, and to the formation, also in Europe, of multi-national markets of sufficient size to allow the establishment of the mass production and distribution techniques characteristic of the large American company.

vision preceded shaped the outcome

The effect was immediate and imposing. The emigration of US capital, which recommenced immediately after the Second World War in the direction of the colonial and semi-colonial world, made a great leap forward in the 1950's, more and more taking the road to Europe and other parts of the world which were either already industrialized or in the process of indus-trialization. Direct US foreign investment, which had contrac-ted from $7.5 billion in 1929 to $7.2 billion in 1946, reached a level of $34.7 bn. in 1961 and $86.0 bn. in 1971. These quantita-tive data conceal an even more important change. In the immediate post-war period, according to the well-known characterization of *Business Week*, the vast majority of the large firms dominating the American economy were 'domestically oriented enterprises with international operations' rather than 'truly world-oriented corporations'.[95] Only in the 1960's did the dynamic component of US capitalism actually acquire a supranational dimension, escaping the control of every nation-state, including that of its country of origin which had prepared and actively supported its post-war expansion.

> In the course of expanding their foreign assets and operations in this spectacular way most of the corporate giants which dominate the US economy . . . have become, in *Business Week's* terminology, multinational corporations. It is not enough that a multinational corporation should have a base of operation abroad; its true *differentia specifica* is that 'its management makes fundamental decisions on marketing, production and research in terms of alternatives that are available to it anywhere in the world'. . . . One cannot say of the giant multinational company of today that it is primarily interested, like the industrialist of the 19th century, in the export of commodities, or, like the banker of the early 20th century, in the export of capital. . . . The only valid generalization one can make is that in every case they will seek a solution which maximizes the (long-run) profits of the enterprise as a whole. This of course means that whenever necessary to the furtherance of this goal, the interests of particular subsidiaries and countries will be ruthlessly sacrificed.[96]

It is not only the national interests of weaker countries that have been subordinated to the interests of the multinational company:

> These giant enterprises are [no] more concerned to promote the national interests of the advanced countries, including even the one in which their headquarters are situated. Quite apart from individual actions – like the Ford Motor Company's remittance abroad of several hundred million dollars to buy out the minority interest of Ford of Britain at a time when the US government was expressing serious concern about the state of the country's balance

---

[95] P. A. Baran and P. M. Sweezy, 'Notes on the Theory of Imperialism' in *Problems of Economic Dynamics and Planning: Essays in Honour of Michal Kalecki*, Warsaw 1966, p. 19.

[96] Ibid., pp. 20–1.

of payments – a plausible argument could be made that in the last fifteen years US corporations have developed their foreign operations at the expense of, and often in competition with, their domestic operations and that these policies have constituted one of the causes of the lagging growth rate of the US economy.[97]

Such a conflict of interests between the large multinational companies and the nation-states in which they originated has been rather more than a mere theoretical possibility. Thus, ever since the end of the 1950's (that is, well before the escalation of the war in Vietnam) the 'emigration' of the giant corporations has thrown into crisis US financial supremacy over Europe,[98] thereby shaking one of the pillars on which the American formal empire had been built (§16). It was already too late when, at the end of 1967, Johnson tried to run for cover in a sharply deteriorating financial situation – when, that is, he limited capital investment abroad, effectively prohibiting any such movements for 1968 to continental Europe and the industrialized countries, and demanding repatriation of American profits. Unleashed by the American imperial order, the supranational economic forces had at last won a certain degree of autonomy, which would inevitably ricochet against any attempt to tamper with them.

In fact, the profits of American firms operating abroad, far from being repatriated, precipitated those speculative pressures on the dollar and other currencies which, within three years, would explode the monetary system established at Bretton Woods. Of course, the crisis was not the work only of the speculative-financial manoeuvres of the US-based multinationals. In fact, the *Pax Americana* had provoked, above all in the 1960's, a competitive reaction to the emigration of the US corporations, causing similar tendencies to appear in Europe and other industrialized regions. At the end of the decade, the mass of capital which had acquired the character of supranationality and which 'behaved' accordingly was much larger than that suggested by the already huge figures relating

[97] Ibid., p. 23.
[98] Cf. R. F. Harrod, *Money*, London 1969, pp. 274–5.

to direct US foreign investment and comparative profit flows.

Released in the economic-monetary field by the activities of
the multinationals, the tendencies working to disintegrate the
old formal order later interacted with those released in the
politico-military field by the nationalism of the imperialized
areas (§16). I am referring, of course, to the increased income of
countries producing industrial raw materials, as a result of the
shift in the relationship of forces between the Third World and
the imperial states. A by no means negligible part of this income
has served as a 'sounding-board' for the tendencies released by
the multinationals, and thus forced the pace at which the
formal Free World empire has passed into the informal empire
of free enterprise.

24. The following question arises naturally at this point. How
can we represent these diverse tendencies – which define the
supranational character of the large contemporary capitalist
firm – in the terms of the three-dimensional grid of Fig. 13?
From what has been said in the last section, it is immediately
apparent that such a representation is not in fact possible.

We have seen first of all that the Keynesian revolution involved the assumption by American imperialism of certain
characteristic trends of the preceding phase of nationalist
imperialism – that is, principally, reversal of the tendency to
underconsumption, and more rigid state control over the supply
and demand of money-capital. It follows that the 'dissolution'
of the space defined by NS $\rightarrow$ F – a process set off by the situation of world-wide anarchy and war (§21) – did not come to a
halt when that situation was overcome after World War Two.
It is not possible, then, to show the characteristic tendencies of
multinational capitalism within the space defined by NS $\rightarrow$ F,
for the simple reason that the tendencies designated by this
arrow are no longer empirically observable.

Furthermore, we have seen that the rise of multinational
capitalism was fuelled on the one hand by the tendency to
anarchy and war which marked inter-state relations in the
first half of this century, and on the other by the tendency to
hierarchical order and peace among states which characterized

Fig. 15

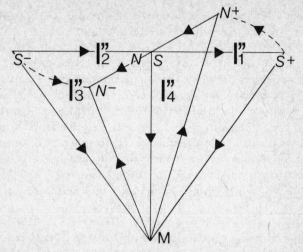

the period after the Second World War. Unlike finance capitalism, then, multinational capitalism must be designated not by means of arrows converging at S^+ and S^- (Fig. 13), but by means of arrows diverging from these same points. This is expressed in Fig. 15, where $S^+ \rightarrow M$ and $S^- \rightarrow M$ designate precisely those two tendencies which fuelled the rise of multinational capitalism (M). The two arrows $M \rightarrow N^-$ and $M \rightarrow N^+$ may be assumed to represent two tendencies which have been fostered by the multinationals themselves: the former, the tendency to promote the formation of wide free-trade areas and, above all, maximum international freedom of circulation of entrepreneurial activity; the latter, a tendency to which we have made only passing allusion in previous sections, but which occupied an important place in Marxist and radical literature of the 60's. I refer to the image of 'neo-colonialism', according to which the multinational expansion of the giant capitalist corporation has tended to consolidate, or to re-create, the typical structures of colonial exploitation – even in situations where, formally speaking, they have long since ceased to exist.

In the 1950s the international monopoly corporation went beyond the simple installation of foreign industry inside Latin American protective tariff walls, which guarantee high prices and profits. First, the foreign assembly plant and merchandizing organization set up a sort of a putting-out system, in which Latin American medium and small manufacturers produce parts for local assembly by the metropolitan monopoly, who prescribes their industrial processes, determines their output, is their only buyer of the same, reduces its own capital expenditure by relying on the investment and credit of its Latin American contractors and sub-contractors, and shift the costs and losses of ... excess capacity on these Latin American manufacturers, while keeping the lion's share of the profit from this arrangement to itself for re-investment and expansion in Latin America or for remission to the metropolis and other parts of its world-wide operation.

In recent years, the metropolitan monopolies have carried this process of metropolitan-satellite integration a step further by associating themselves with Latin American industrial and/or financial groups or even public institutions in so-called mixed enterprises. ... The metropolitan corporation's main contribution to the joint enterprise ... is a technological package of patents, designs, industrial processes, high-salaries technicians and, last but not least, trademarks and salesmanship. ... The international monopoly corporation then proceeds to take full advantage of its technological monopoly, its financial reserve, and its direct or indirect political power, to draw increasingly more profits than its Latin American partners out of the common enterprise, sector, economy, and country of Latin America in which it operates. ... Everywhere – in the capitalist world, that is – American technology is becoming the new source of monopoly power and the new basis of economic colonialism and political neo-colonialism.[99]

Multinational capitalism is thus designated in Fig. 15 by means of an ensemble of tendencies which bring into relief its 'contradictory' character (in the sense that it originates in tendencies of an opposite matrix – $S^- \rightarrow M$ and $S^+ \rightarrow M$ – and that it in turn fosters opposite tendencies – $M \rightarrow N^+$ and $M \rightarrow N^-$). There is a certain formal similarity between this contradictory character and that which marked finance capitalism in our analysis above. But, as a comparison of Figs. 13 and 15 shows at once, the analogy conceals a substantive difference – whereas high finance, not being intrinsically endowed with

[99] A. G. Frank, *Capitalism and Underdevelopment in Latin America*, New York and London 1969, pp. 299–304.

competitive capacity, tended to promote expansion of the state
$(F \rightarrow S^+$ and $F \rightarrow S^-)$ the big multinational company, which is
so endowed, tends instead to foster expansion of the nation
$(M \rightarrow N^+$ and $M \rightarrow N^-)$, in the widest meaning of the nation as
a 'culture' embodied in goods and ideas.

In his way, Hobson himself seemed to be aware of this difference. For, towards the end of his study, he warned the reader
of a possible confusion between the concept of international
finance (with which he had dealt) and the phenomenon of direct
investment which was beginning to develop at the very time
when he was writing:

> The forces of international finance are commonly described as
> capitalistic, but the gravest danger arises not from genuine indus-
> trial investments in foreign lands, but from the handling of stocks
> and shares based upon these investments by financiers. Those who
> own a genuine state in the natural sources or the industry of a
> foreign land have at least some substantial interest in the peace
> and good government of that land; but the stock speculator has no
> such stake; his interest lies in the oscillations of paper values, which
> require fluctuation and insecurity of political conditions as their
> instrument.[100]

However, finance capitalism and multinational capitalism are
not only distinct concepts; they are also opposites. Of course,
large firms operating on a multinational scale are nothing new
in the history of capitalism. The big merchant companies, for
example, may even be considered as, in certain respects, the
progenitors of high finance (§22). But neither these firms nor the
great mining companies and plantations which made possible
their commerce may be regarded as the forerunners of the
present-day multinational companies. As Hymer has pointed
out:

> They were like dinosaurs, large in bulk, but small in brain, feeding
> on the lush vegetation of the new worlds (the planters and miners
> in America were literally *Tyrannosaurus rex*).[101]

[100] Hobson, op. cit., p. 359.
[101] Hymer, op. cit.

To be more precise, the fundamental difference between the great merchant companies of the past and high finance on the one hand, and the multinational companies on the other, lies in their respective relationships to the international division of labour: while the former influenced it in a mediated and indirect manner, the latter do so in an immediate and direct way. This differential relationship corresponds *grosso modo* to the distinction between *market* and *company* (or workplace) as *opposite* modes of co-ordination of the division of labour: on the market, this co-ordination occurs 'anarchically' and informally; in the company, 'hierarchically' and formally.

Above all, once it enters the phase of 'intensive' expansion (§23), the big multinational company promotes its own more or less advanced internal division of labour, which tends to cut across the territorial division of the world into states and nations. High finance and its progenitors (the big merchant companies), far from developing within themselves an international division of labour, owed their very existence to the division of the world into separate national entities, each with its internal division of labour. They thereby had an influence upon the way in which the various productive activities were distributed among the nations; but it was an indirect influence, exerted through market forces and mediated, to a greater or lesser extent, by inter-state relations. Finance capitalism and multinational capitalism are thus antithetical concepts, in that the former represents an 'anarchic-informal' mode, and the latter a 'hierarchical-formal' mode, of co-ordination of the international division of labour.[102]

The above distinction becomes more precise once we define the significance of the arrow NS → M. Because of its central position within the system represented by Fig. 15, this arrow should be given the role of 'tap-root' of multinational capitalism. It will be recalled (§20) that the tendency to underconsump-

---

[102] This does not imply that the former lacks any 'order' while the latter is perfectly endowed with it. It simply means that, in the first case, order is produced outside the firm by impersonal forces (Adam Smith's 'invisible hand') while in the second case, it is an objective consciously pursued, but not necessarily attained, within the firm itself.

tion, which was the tap-root of finance imperialism, was attributed by Hobson to the fact that competition tended to keep wages tied to the cost of living, preventing them from rising in step with productivity. While correct, this judgment is limited to one of the two aspects of the relationship between capitalist accumulation and distribution of the social product. If we consider the relationship from the side of the ownership, or rather control, of the means of production, and the *market* balance of forces between Capital and Labour, then capitalist accumulation undoubtedly appears as a process whereby such control is progressively concentrated in the hands of 'a few' and the bargaining power of Labour is correspondingly weakened. But if we look at this same relationship from another side – that of the relations between Capital and Labour *within the firm* or workplace – then we are led to draw opposite conclusions. Indeed, it is becoming more and more evident that capitalist accumulation, by depersonalizing and draining of all professional content a growing proportion of 'factory labour', tends to increase the 'unruliness' of the labour force *to the very extent that it makes such unruliness more costly*, owing to the intensified division of labour and the greater quantity of capital invested in the productive process.

Now, it seems to me that it is precisely this second tendency which constitutes the 'tap-root' of multinational capitalism. For what could more effectively restore company profit margins, lowered by the unruliness of the labour force, than the decentralization of production? Indeed once its dimensions, internal division of labour, and capital investment have reached a certain level, a company can only re-establish the internal hierarchical order so necessary for its functioning by organizing its productive and distributive operations at a world level. NS $\rightarrow$ M designates precisely this tendency of the large company to expand on a multinational scale, in order to escape the decline of the rate of profit in the 'mother-country'.

That this is not the only root of the phenomenon should be clear from what was said above and from the very representation of Fig. 15, where NS $\rightarrow$ M converges at M with $S^+ \rightarrow$ M and $S^- \rightarrow$ M. It is perhaps worth explaining, however, that the opposition between the two characteristic tendencies of capitalist accumulation – that of underconsumption/overproduction and that of the falling rate of profit – does not rule out the possibility of their coexistence and interaction. Quite the contrary. In a certain sense, each of the two actually implies the other: the tendency to underconsumption, by impeding the transformation of commodity-capital into money-capital, always involves a fall in the rate of profit; while the tendency of company profit margins to be squeezed, by discouraging investment, always involves a reduction of effective demand and the appearance of phenomena of overproduction. From this point of view, the two tendencies may have identical external manifestations: a fall in the rate of profit and a rise in unutilized productive capacity. This accounts for the difficulties generally encountered in distinguishing between the two types of tendency on the basis of an estimation of the level of the rate of profit and of productive capacity employed. As a matter of fact, it is impossible to draw a distinction on that basis: only by assessing the actual relationship of forces between Labour and Capital in the firm (or workplace), and its 'imperviousness' to market fluctuations, is it possible to determine which of the two tendencies should be considered the 'cause' and which the 'effect'.

My own estimate is as follows. Up to the end of the last century, the principal tendency was that of underconsumption – which substantially confirms Hobson's judgment designated by NS → F in Fig. 13. But since then the relationship between the two has been progressively reversed, so that the tendency of company profit margins to be squeezed has finally become the predominant one. The shift of the epicentre of world concentration from England to the United States, the sharp rise in capitalist accumulation connected to this shift and to the thirty years of war economy which accompanied it, the implementation of so-called scientific management or Taylorism, and the Keynesian revolution mentioned above – these have been the principal phenomena contributing to the reversal.[103]

_____

[103] I realize that, unlike previous evaluations, this conjecture cannot be

We have now completed our definition of multinational capitalism as an ensemble of tendencies antithetical to the ensemble in terms of which we defined finance imperialism. The two ensembles are represented together in Fig. 16 in order to provide a visual image of their opposition and to facilitate analysis of their differences. The reader is free at this point to use his own imagination in drawing a synchronic and dia-chronic specification of the various sub-ensembles which make up multinational capitalism. These would show that the analogies made in the last chapter were simply the result of the attempt to flatten in a two-dimensional plane a number of tendencies which, in a three-dimensional analysis, are located in quite distinct ensembles.

So far as the aims of this essay are concerned, two observations should be sufficient. First, it should be noted that 18th and 19th century English imperialism, and American imperialism after the Second World War (represented in Fig 16 by the paths $NS \rightarrow N^+ \rightarrow S^-$ and $NS \rightarrow S^- \rightarrow N^-$ respectively), not only have diverse origins (one in quadrant I_1, the other in quadrant I_2, as we saw in previous chapters) but, more fundamentally, move in distinct spaces. They differ in respect both of the 'field of forces' to which they belong – if I may be permitted the metaphor – and of their point of convergence. As the reader may easily ascertain from either Fig. 15 or Fig. 16, the definition we have given of multinational capitalism actually produces convergence at N^-, rather than at the point S^+, implied by Hobson's definition of finance imperialism. If these definitions are judicious, it follows that whereas 19th century English formal imperialism was an unstable phenomenon destined to pass into a state of universal anarchy and war, the informal American imperialism

taken as a generally accepted fact. It is not even, indeed perhaps least of all, acknowledged among Marxist scholars. It is introduced here solely to underline the opposition between the ideal types of 'finance capitalism' and 'multinational capitalism': that is, to indicate the direction of hypotheses which will illuminate, rather than occlude, the anomalous character of multinational capitalism with respect to Hobson's concept of imperialism. Although it has been scarcely explored, this field of research has already been broached by a number of scholars. (Cf. F. Gambino, 'Composizione di classe e investimenti diretti statunitensi all'estero' in Ferrari Bravo (ed.) op. cit.)

Fig. 16

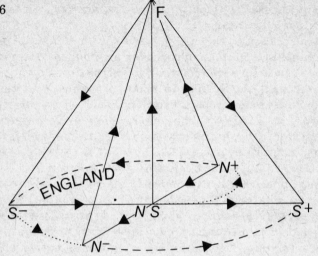

Fig. 16—

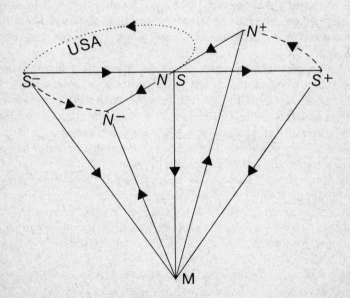

which has asserted itself in the last decade represents a relatively *stable* tendency.

I say 'relatively' because the grid within which the present tendencies of American imperialism are defined does not itself have much assurance of stability. This is, in fact, the second observation I should like to make. We know that the convergence of finance imperialism at S^+ involved a reversal of the tendency to underconsumption ($NS \rightarrow F$) and, consequently, 'dissolution' of the entire ensemble of tendencies which defined finance capitalism itself (§21–23). What is the implication of convergence at N^- for the stability of the grid? It should be noted at once that convergence of the system at N^- does not involve a reversal of the tendency of company profit margins to be squeezed ($NS \rightarrow M$), to which we have attributed the role of 'tap-root' of multinational capitalism. It is true that, in the short term, freer international circulation of entrepreneurial activity may determine a relative weakening of Labour against Capital in those countries and areas where the drive to multinationalism has its origin. It is also true, however, that, in the medium to long term, fulfilment of this drive cannot but increase capitalist concentration and the division of labour on a global scale, thereby ultimately shifting the relationship of forces between Labour and Capital to the advantage of the former.

Although convergence at N^- does not imply a reversal of the tendency of company profit margins to be squeezed, or of the resultant 'dissolution' of the ensemble of tendencies which define multinational capitalism, nevertheless it does involve a weakening of the nation-state as the primary structure of the international system. Growing freedom of the international circulation of entrepreneurial activity, together with its corollary, freer circulation of goods and ideas, increases the homogeneity and interdependence of nations – a phenomenon which in the end overshadows their character as separate and mutually exclusive realities (§5). The entire conceptual plane defined by expansion of the nation-state (that is, by the coordinates $N^+ \rightarrow NS \rightarrow N^-$ and $S^+ \rightarrow NS \rightarrow S^-$) on which Hobson's definition of imperialism was based, thus tends to lose all relevance and, in that sense, 'dissolves away'.

me: why doesn't matter if its Carter or Reagan or Volcker is key

Reagan has vastly increased state expenditure (military) w/o real result; Volcker has got result

Concluding Remarks

In conclusion, let us reconsider the quotation from *Imperialism: A Study* with which we began this essay. To define an 'ism' has proved an extremely arduous, although not impossible, task. The kind of problem which, in the natural sciences, presents itself with full clarity only at the level of 'the infinitely large' or 'the infinitely small', arises immediately in the social sciences whatever the object of investigation. The impalpability of a phenomenon like imperialism to the world of our senses heightens the dependence of our definition on the type of conceptual grid by means of which we attempt to order both historical events and the tendencies normally associated with them.

The very signifier 'imperialism' has been, and still is, used to designate diverse, and in certain respects antithetical, ensembles of tendencies. Identification of these discrete meanings presupposes that we define, by means of a series of distinctions and oppositions, a conceptual grid capable of synchronically and diachronically ordering the more general facts to which the term refers. In Chapter 1, we saw that superimposition of a one-dimensional grid on the empirical data makes it possible to attribute a linear order to them, but that this order varies according to the grid employed. If two are combined in a single two-dimensional grid, the order becomes circular, and the four significations I_1, I_2, I_3 and I_4 may be attributed to imperialism either simultaneously or successively (Chapter 2). In Chapter 3, we showed that by the usage of a series of analogies we can assign a recurrent, as well as circular, order to the tendencies of imperialism. But this recurrence and circularity depend entirely on the two-dimensional character of the grid in question. If a third dimension is introduced, as in Chapter 4, then the recurrence is dissolved and the four significations I_1, I_2, I_3 and I_4 are separated into ensembles with opposite meanings.

By proceeding in this way, we can introduce new dimensions or articulations, define ever more complex orders, and multiply at will the number of significations which are, or can be, attributed to the term 'imperialism'. It is not necessary to do this, however, in order to become aware of the *two-fold relativity* of every definition of imperialism. As a matter of fact, any definition will always depend on a two-fold choice: that of an ideotypical grid or structure, and that of a position (for example, I_4) within the grid itself.

For anyone who places himself on the terrain of scientific research, the respective options actually taken must be answerable to the criterion of empirical relevance – that is to say, they must be able to give a univocal representation of factual data which are generally held to be relevant. Every definition, then, has to be repeatedly subjected to empirical control, that is, not only constant observation of the real world, of a more or less 'participatory' character according to the field of observation, but also and especially continual specification and articulation of the conceptual apparatus for alerting the observer to the appearance of anomalies.

The importance of such alertness to the appearance of anomalies is still greater in the social sciences than it normally is in the natural sciences. In fact, the former are not only characterized by their relative lack of genuine paradigms – that is scientific achievements which, at a given moment, provide *everyone* involved in a certain research field with a model of the range of acceptable problems and solutions. Even those of their theoretical constructs which come closest to the status of paradigm have a greater degree of transience. As Weber pointed out: 'There are sciences to which eternal youth is granted – all those to which the eternally onward flowing stream of culture perpetually brings new problems. At the very heart of their task lies not only the transiency of *all* ideal types, *but* also at the same time the inevitability of *new* ones. The intellectual apparatus which the past has developed through the analysis, or more truthfully, the analytical rearrangement of the immediately given reality, and through the latter's integration by concepts which correspond to the state of its knowledge and the focus of its interest, is in constant tension with the new knowledge which we can and *desire* to wrest from reality. The progress of cultural science occurs through this conflict. Its result is the perpetual reconstruction of those concepts through which we seek to comprehend reality. The history of the social sciences is and remains a continuous process passing from the attempt to order reality analytically through the construction of concepts – the dissolution of the analytical constructs so constructed through the expansion and shift of the scientific horizon – and the reformulation anew of concepts on the foundations thus transformed'.[104]

Analysis of Hobson's ideo-typical structure has demonstrated the validity of these observations. Thus, we have seen how rigidly circumscribed in time is the capacity of such a structure to order expansionist phenomena synchronically and diachronically. This capacity is zero for phenomena prior to the second half of the 17th century – that is, before the nation-state began to exercise a decisive influence over the international system; it is maximal for phenomena of the late 19th century, when the nation-state had finally become the basic structure of the international system; while its very application is dubious to times of crisis of the nation-state, such as those in which we seem to live.

The limits of Hobson's 'paradigm' become still more apparent once we scrutinize the relationship of sufficient causation it postulated between imperialism and capitalism. We have already seen that the so-called multinationalization of capital represents an anomaly of such radical proportions for Hobson's ideo-typical structure that it strikes at its foundations. On the one hand, that structure cannot comprehend (that is, order within its own field) the empirical development which is

---

[104] Weber, op. cit., pp. 104–5.

generally considered to be one of the most significant features
of post-war capitalism. On the other hand, if we redefine the
tendencies to which Hobson referred when he spoke of 'imperialism' to cover this anomaly, we discover that the point of
convergence of the system so defined not only diverges from
that hypothesized by Hobson, but also represents a transcen-
dence of that division of the world into nation-states which
formed the analytical origin of Hobson's entire construction.

I am not denying, of course, that expansionist forces are at
work today and that they may issue in a new world war. But
although such tendencies are present in reality, they fall outside Hobson's schema of interpretation – that is to say, they are
extraneous to the connection between 'imperialism' and
'capitalism' that characterized the schema in an original and
specific manner. It is precisely in this sense that Hobson's ideo-
typical structure 'dissolves' or loses relevance as an interpretative schema of the phenomena termed imperialist.

It is thus anachronistic for a scientific investigation to
attempt to ground a theory of contemporary imperialism in
historically determinate definitions which relate to processes
and ideologies of the first decades of this century. If our introductory remarks on the relationship between Hobson and
Lenin are borne in mind, it should be perfectly clear that this
conclusion, which is based on an examination of the theory of
the former, is *a fortiori* valid for those of its definitions which
are preserved in the theory of the latter. However, at the risk of
introducing new misunderstandings, one last point may profit-
ably be specified.

It is true that this essay has not furnished an exhaustive and
univocal representation of Lenin's concept of imperialism. In
fact, this concept is erected on two theoretical constructions –
that of Hobson and that of Hilferding – which are not only distinct, but even *incommensurable*, in that they cannot be reduced
to a single ideo-typical structure. In our introduction, we
alluded to the fact that the concepts of 'finance capital' employed by Hilferding and Hobson, while designated by means
of the same signifier, have virtually nothing to do with each
other (cf. p. 25). We may now add that the *primary* types which

define Hilferding's ideo-typical structure concern not the forms of expansion of state, nation and capital *beyond* the boundaries of the nation-state, but the forms of property and competition present *within* it.[105] In other words, Hilferding's ideo-typical structure represents what appears in Hobson's structure as a point (NS) which forms the analytical origin of the entire structure, but which in itself has neither 'form' nor 'content'. It is in this sense, then, that the two structures are incommensurable.

It follows that our attempt (§§14, 22) to represent Lenin's concept of imperialism within Hobson's 'ideo-typical' structure was necessarily partial and equivocal, since it omitted those components of Lenin's theory that he had derived from Hilferding. Whoever wishes to construct an exhaustive and univocal representation of Lenin's concept of imperialism must therefore first reconstruct the ideo-typical structure presupposed by Hilferding's theory of finance capital. That is not necessary, however, if we intend, more modestly to show only the historical relativity of that concept. It will then be sufficient to show, as I have tried to do in this essay, that *at least one* of its two theoretical presuppositions has no significance (that is, relevance) for the contemporary world.

The potential incommensurability of different theories of imperialism is a reminder that this essay is only a first step along a wholly unexplored path. For example, the incommensurability of the theories of Hobson and Hilferding is such that if we had explicated the ideo-typical structure presupposed by the latter, we would have obtained a representation of imperialism quite different from that expounded in this essay. Moreover, other representations, partially or completely distinct from either of these, would be obtained by a reconstruction of the ideo-typical structures implicit in the theories of Luxemburg, Bukharin or Schumpeter – to mention only those which have exercised a major influence, directly or indirectly, on modern theories of imperialism.

The reconstruction of a plurality of ideo-typical structures

---

[105] See R. Hilferding, *Das Finanzkapital*, Vienna 1923.

would indeed perhaps be the best remedy to the lacunae of the schematic representation contained in this essay – so long as it is not further complicated by the insertion of new dimensions or articulations. I said at the end of the introduction that the omissions and schematisms of my study were due not only to the need to keep the puzzle within the limits of my solving power. They also expressed my assessment of how best to construct a univocal representation of Hobson's ideo-typical structure without at the same time 'doing violence to reality'. Thus when I decided, in Chapters 2 and 3, to limit my analysis to the imperialism of the hegemonic powers, I did so on the grounds that such a restriction would render the representation more precise and univocal. By contrast when I decided, in Chapter 4, to abandon the representation of the socio-economic forces present within the hegemonic nation-state, immediately after introducing it, I did so on the grounds that the three co-ordinates which correspond to the expansion of the state, nation (or ethnicity) and capital, exhaustively define Hobson's ideo-typical structure; and that all the other components of the imperialist phenomenon either were accessory and negligible elements of that structure, or else could be represented in the space defined by these three co-ordinates and their articulation (§§19–20).

In short, my view is that integration of the social dimension (or any other that I have not examined) into a representation of imperialism, without formalism and without 'doing violence to reality', demands that we leave Hobson's ideo-typical structure, to reconstruct or construct *ex novo* other conceptual spaces that correspond to other points of view. But such an ulterior procedure will itself never be able to remedy *all* lacunae and eliminate *all* schematism in an attempt to reconstruct 'the real'. A construction of that kind would be so complicated that it could never be utilized. The only meaningful goal of such an endeavour will be the creation of a *symbolic* order within which it may finally be possible to inter-relate diverse theoretical positions and perhaps even to render them commensurable.

Afterword

Comments and criticisms by reviewers[1], colleagues, students and friends since the book was first published have convinced me that I have not been sufficiently clear and explicit about the purpose and scope of the *Geometry*. In this Afterword I shall therefore try first of all to dispel the main misunderstandings I have come across. I will then try to meet some of the criticisms proper and point out what, in my opinion, is the continuing relevance of the book.*

I

Many have seen in the *Geometry* a new theory of Imperialism. This is surprising to me since I stated several times in the book that I was not offering any new theory but merely a reconstruction of an existing theory (see, e.g., pp. 10, 33). The mis-

[1] The reviewers I am explicitly or implicitly referring to in what follows are B. Semmel in *New Left Review*, 118, 1979, pp. 73–79; B. Jossa in *Studi Economici*, 1979, pp. 131–157; F. Block in *Contemporary Sociology*, viii, 5, 1979, pp. 757–758; A. Phillips in *Capital and Class*, 9, 1979, pp. 139–141; A. Bagchi, 'A note on the requirements of a theory of imperialism', paper presented at the annual colloquium sponsored by the Max Plank Institut (Starnberg), Fernand Braudel Center (Binghamton) and Maison des Sciences de l'Homme (Paris), Starnberg June 1980; J. Willoughby in *Science and Society*, XLV, 4, 1981–82, pp. 491–494; R. Mukherjee in *Review*, VI, 4, 1983. This Afterword draws heavily from my answer to Mukherjee to be published in the same issue of *Review*.

* I would like to thank T. K. Hopkins, W. G. Martin and B. J. Silver for their helpful comments on an earlier draft.

understanding has probably arisen from the difficulties involved in distinguishing the construction from the reconstruction of a theory. By the latter I mean making explicit and submitting to careful analysis what was tacitly taken for granted, unknowingly presumed, or simply considered too obvious even to note in passing by those who originally advanced the versions of the theory under examination. I mean uncovering the unexplicated *premises* of a theory with a view to assess their empirical/historical *relevance*. It thus differs sharply from what might be called theory construction which involves stating premises, deriving *hypotheses* and proceding to specify forms for assessing their empirical/historical *validity*. In practice, the two exercises may of course overlap. Procedurally, however, they are very different kinds of operations. And while theory reconstruction may often be but a preface to a work of theory construction, in some instances it takes priority over the latter in the sense that it stands by itself, independently of such efforts at theory construction that may follow upon it.

I shall later explain in which way the *Geometry* may be considered a preface to a theory of world-hegemony. But quite independently of any such possibility, it is first and foremost an explication of the premises of extant theory of imperialism, with the aim of assessing its empirical/historical relevance. The reasons for my giving priority to theory reconstruction over theory construction, I stated in the Introduction. But I did so in an admittedly rather oblique way, and so let me restate them here more explicitly and directly.

By the early 1970s, when the book was first conceived, two main bodies of analysis had developed, which were quite distinct in their premises but confusingly lumped together under the label 'theories of imperialism'. The first body of theories, produced from the beginning of the century up through the First World War, had a common object of analysis: the growing competition by capitalist states over territory. The various social scientists and political practitioners that contributed to the construction of this body of theories gave different explanations for such competition and projected different outcomes from its unfolding. The most famous controversy was that between Lenin and Kautsky. Yet, like everyone else involved in the debate – with the possible partial exception of Luxemburg and Schumpeter – they were talking about and analysing the same thing: the growing competition over territory among capitalist states.[2] Moreover, they even agreed on the main cause of the phenomenon: the growing trustification of capital. As the passage I quote at p. 15 of the Introduction clearly shows, they differed principally only on the likely outcome of the process of trustification. Kautsky, on the one hand, believed that the process would produce a single world trust and a corresponding stage of 'ultra-imperialism' (a peaceful world union of capitalist states); Lenin, on the other hand, maintained that the process of trustification, by heightening rather than diminishing uneven development among capitalist states, would strengthen the tendency toward war and revolution.

Since both critics sympathetic to my account (such as Semmel) and critics not so sympathetic to it (such as Willoughby) have seen in the *Geometry* an attempt to resurrect Kautsky's theory of ultra-imperialism, I shall later come back to this matter. For the time being, I just want to point out that, from within this problematic of world-conditions, World War Two was the second and in the event final instalment of the process of war that settled, by reframing, the question at issue in the competition among capitalist states for territory that had begun in the latter part of the nineteenth century. For with the end of World War Two this kind of competition was literally eliminated from the world-scene. Displacing and replacing it was the complex of developmental processes through which US hegemony was rapidly established and – in due course – would also be slowly eroded. The 1950's and 1960's thus saw a reversal of the historical tendencies that had characterized the world system from the end of the nineteenth century through the

---

[2] R. Luxemburg emphasizes just as much, if not more, the struggle of capitalism against what she calls the natural economy, while J. Schumpeter emphasizes the propensity of state structures towards unlimited territorial expansion. Cf R. Luxemburg, *The Accumulation of Capital*, London 1963 and J. Schumpeter, *Imperialism – Social Classes*, New York 1955.

1930's, tendencies that had given rise to and been the object of the 'classical' theories of imperialism: the unity of the world market – the one that British hegemony had formed and that was disintegrated by the growing opposition to and consequent decline of British power, a decomposition that reached its nadir in the 1930's – was largely reconstituted; and capitalist competition correspondingly shifted back from the political arena of inter-state relations to the economic arena of inter-enterprise relations.

There was a second body of theories. In the same period, the 1950's and 1960's, and so well after the factual premises of the classical body of theories of imperialism were being historically eliminated, political and intellectual opposition to past and continuing relations between the evidently developed and the evidently much less developed countries, grew. And so did theories expressing this opposition and explaining historically and analytically why such relations not only had in the past enriched the rich and exploited the poor among the countries of the world but were doing so now as well and, *ceteris paribus*, would continue to do in the future. This body of theories was also called theories of imperialism, despite its emergence with premises quite different from those of the earlier body. Here the emphasis was on domination and its reciprocal, dependence, rather than competition and war. This shift of emphasis was of course fully justified by the changed political-economic circumstances within which world capitalism would have to operate after the Second World War. Even retaining the term imperialism to designate the new conjuncture could be justified on the definitional ground that a combination of domination and competition at the level of both the inter-state system and the world market had always characterized capitalism.

There were, however, two main problems with this change of premises. In the first place, if it is true that world capitalism has always been characterized by a combination of domination and competition, then it is not clear what purpose a theory of imperialism, one distinct from a theory of world capitalism pure and simple, may serve. The classical theories of imperialism did have such an independent or specific purpose, precisely because

[left margin, handwritten:] cf. Polanyi's snapping of golden thread

of their presupposition that world capitalism had entered a new stage, one in which competition among states over territory had become the principal contradiction of world capitalist relations and the one which would result in the exhaustion of the contending bourgeoisies. They were theories of and for this particular stage. However, if theories of imperialism also come to cover a stage in which competition is once again within an inter-enterprise arena, and domination of peripheral by core countries, let us say, has become the principal contradiction of world capitalist relations, then all the specificity of those theories, relative to a theory of world capitalism, is lost.

This problem was compounded by a second one. The quite different premises of the two bodies of theories were not made explicit and carefully analyzed in their implications. On the contrary, the differences in the premises were ignored, over-looked, downplayed, or misapprehended in the emphasis on elements of supposed continuity in the patterns of competition and domination from the end of the nineteenth century up to the present. Paradigmatic, from this point of view, has been the emphasis on 'monopoly capital'. Originally put forward by some of the early theorists (Lenin in particular) as an explanation of the phenomenon of imperialism, monopoly capital was now turned into the phenomenon itself: imperialism, that is, comes to be identified with the monopoly stage of capitalism.

As a result, much of the debate on imperialism that developed in the late 1960's and early 1970's was vitiated by basic misunderstandings over the very object of the debate. To some, imperialism still meant military competition among advanced capitalist states; to others it meant domination in the capitalist world-economy; to still others it meant a particular stage of capitalism – just to mention three of the several positions taken in the debate.

Along with others I was disturbed by this loss of a common language of discourse. It seemed to me therefore that what was required was not a new theory of imperialism (imperialism as what? anyway) but a careful analysis of the premises of existing theories in order to show their boundaries in relation, one, to each other and, two, to the constant flow of new historical data.

More specifically, it seemed to me that what was most required was to show that the classical body of theories of imperialism as a whole, irrespective of the scientific merits and demerits of any one of them, had become irrelevant as outlines for interpretative accounts of world-historical events, trends, and developmental tendencies since the Second World War.

By way of illustration let us go back to the Lenin-Kautsky controversy referred to above. As I point out both in the Introduction and in Chapter III (pp. 15–16, 90–92), if we take the thirty-year period following the publication of Lenin's pamphlet, his assessment of world-capitalist tendencies was undoubtedly more valid than Kautsky's. The establishment of the *pax Americana* after World War II did not make Kautsky's theory more valid than Lenin's. Rather, it made them *both irrelevant.* For the *pax Americana* was not the outcome of the creation of a single world trust as held by Kautsky's theory. Paradoxically, its establishment owed more to the *partial* fulfillment of Lenin's expectations: socialist revolution, a new world war and revolutionary upheaval in colonial and semi-colonial countries. Once established, however, not only did the *pax Americana* fail to rest on the consolidation of state monopolistic tendencies, as Kautsky had projected, but it also failed to look like a mere 'truce' between wars among capitalist states, as Lenin had projected. Rather, it came to rest on the re-establishment of competition in the economic arena of inter-enterprise relations in a way that made it analogous, though far from identical, to the *pax Britannica* of the nineteenth century.

As a consequence, the common premises of Lenin's and Kautsky's theories of imperialism (growing competition over territory among capitalist states associated with a growing trustification of capital) simply vanished historically: the question of whether one or the other were valid, with reference to 'the imperialism of the 1960s', became a bit like the question of whether 'the present king of France' were bald or not. This, in a nutshell, is what the *Geometry* has to say concerning the Lenin-Kautsky controversy.

In order to show the irrelevance of the classical body of theories of imperialism as a whole for recent conditions and trends, irrespective of the scientific merits and demerits of any one of them, I chose a theoretical referent and a form of theoretical representation that would allow me to explicate the common premises of such theories in as precise a manner as possible. Though my target was Lenin, I chose J. A. Hobson's *Imperialism* as a theoretical referent. The criticism voiced by some reviewers (Phillips, Willoughby, Bagchi) that I have paid too little attention to the Hobson-Lenin relationship would have some validity if my concern was to assess the scientific merits of their respective theories. However, since my main concern was with the relevance of their common premises, I have nothing to add to what is stated in the Introduction (particularly at pp. 23–26) except to emphasize the fact that Hobson paid far more attention than any of the other classical theorists to the problem of defining the object of enquiry. Indeed, the quotation from Hobson with which I open the first chapter (p. 35) could be taken, *mutatis mutandis*, to illustrate the very situation we were facing seventy years later.

The problem he faced was that of distinguishing the phenomenon of Imperialism as it manifested itself in his time from the idea of Empire (a hierarchcical order of states guaranteeing universal peace) that had traditionally been synonymous with internationalism. The problem we faced in the early 1970's was that of distinguishing the phenomenon Hobson and Lenin referred to as Imperialism (the anarchy in inter-state relations arising from the competition among core states over territory) from the phenomenon we referred to as Imperialism (the hierarchical order of states and associated structure of domination, that had come to characterize the capitalist world-economy after the Second World War). In both instances the problem arose from the tendency of political practitioners to obscure, expand or distort the meaning of words, and in each instance the utmost attention was required in defining 'imperialism' as an object of scientific investigation. As I emphasize in the Introduction (pp. 19–22, 26), from this point of view Lenin and Hobson were moving in opposite directions. And whether or not we sympathize with Lenin on political grounds, we must side with Hobson on grounds of scientific rigour.

II

Let us now turn to the form of representation of Hobson's theoretical space. A geometrical metaphor seemed to me the best way of overcoming the confusion connected with purely verbal forms of expression and of making concrete the very idea of theoretical space. It also seemed the most obvious way of representing Hobson's definition, since the series of distinctions through which he was trying to pin down and mark out the particular form of expansionism that he named Imperialism formed two couples of opposites that defined four quadrants in, loosely speaking, a topological space. Only one of these quadrants represented the object of his study. All the others represented forms of expansionism that can and have been loosely referred to as 'imperialism' but that Hobson excluded from the domain of his object of investigation.

My representation has been criticized (mainly by Semmel) on three grounds: 1) that it does not help the reader to understand the text better that he or she might otherwise; 2) that it leads me speciously to distort/restrict the discussion of the issues raised; and 3) that at times it is treated like an instrument of analysis capable of producing conclusions of the order of Cartesian geometry, which it does not and cannot do. Let me try to meet these criticisms by further clarifying the purpose and scope of the book.

It is certainly legitimate to maintain that, in order to appreciate the narrative of a journey one does not need, and indeed might be encumbered by, a set of maps on which the journey can be traced step by step. This will be even more the case if the reader has some idiosyncrasy against maps or has to learn from scratch the keys that will help him or her make sense of them. That this makes map-reading tough going for such a reader is undeniable; but that can hardly be held against the geographer or land-surveyor whose job it is to construct the maps. And that is basically all that I tried to do in the *Geometry*: to construct a map that would help us orient ourselves in the maze of theoretical and historiographical reflections that, at various times, have grown up around accounts of expansionist/imperialist phenomena. Whatever narrative there is in the book, is either an illustration of or a by-product of this mapping endeavour. Hence, by and large, such narrative as there is consists of very well known and very general facts and ideas which by themselves could not possibly make the narrative interesting. If so serious an historian as Semmel, notwithstanding all the criticisms, has found the account interesting, I can only congratulate my maps for having helped me to pull something worth discussing out of rather dull raw material.

For my part, what I minimally wanted to achieve with my maps were three things: 1) a univocal location/classification of the major expansionist tendencies that have characterized the capitalist world-economy before and after the emergence of theories of imperialism; 2) a demonstration that the expansionist tendencies that have come to characterize the capitalist world-economy since the Second World War (and that I argue represent the historical premises of the new body of theories of imperialism), fall completely outside the field of study with which the classical theories were concerned; and 3) an illustration of the fact that the *pax Americana* established after the Second World War had more in common with the *pax Britannica* of the nineteenth century than with what the classical theorists of imperialism were referring to – the latter, in turn, having many more traits in common with the mercantilism of the seventeenth and eighteenth centuries.

In my opinion, the topological space I derived from Hobson performs all these functions reasonably well. Indeed, it helped me – and I hope those who take the trouble to familiarize themselves with its use – to reduce the limitations, ambiguities and inconsistencies of the analogies and counterpositions marking the various theories of imperialism as ordinarily expressed. More specifically, the maps show that we must choose between one of two things. Either current theories of imperialism refer to the *pax Americana* – in which case they refer to an object quite different from that of classical theories and it is therefore advisable to stop referring to their object as imperialism and to stop resorting to explanations that refer to a different object; or they refer to the same object as classical theories – in which case they are totally irrelevant for the study of the capitalist world-economy since the Second World War. For Marxists, they cannot have it both ways. If they stick to the classical definition of imperialism, they have to admit that imperialism was not the *highest* stage of capitalism but a phase in a cycle that since World War II has moved on to a different phase for which they will find no explanation in the received texts. If, on the other hand, they choose to expand the definition of imperialism to include the whole range of possible expansionist tendencies that may occur in a capitalist world-economy, then they have to stop referring to imperialism as a particular stage of capitalism.

In meeting the second criticism (that the diagrammatic representation leads me to distort/restrict speciously the evidence examined and the discussion of the issues raised), I can now distinguish between distortions and restrictions that are a necessary consequence of a given choice of the coordinates and the scale of the maps (given the purpose for which they have been constructed) and distortions/restrictions that are due either to shortcomings of the maps in representing what they are supposed to represent or to my mistakes of classification/location of historical data on the maps. On the inevitability of the first kind of distortions/restrictions, I have really nothing to add to what is already stated in the book (see in particular pp. 30–32, 47–48, 108–110, 151–154). I shall simply illustrate the point with reference to two criticisms, one by Jossa and one by Semmel.

Jossa maintains that the Market/State dichotomy would have been more useful than the elusive Nation/State dichotomy in mapping expansionist phenomena in the capitalist world-economy. Jossa might very well be right and I strongly sympathize with his view. Still, my main concern being to emphasize the distance between the presuppositions of classical and current theories of imperialism, I had no choice but to reconstruct as faithfully as possible the terms of the former. Had I taken other, possibly more interesting theoretical referents, such as Adam Smith (the true forefather of theories of imperialism),[3] the State/Market dichotomy would have been the most obvious one to adopt. This, however, would have taken me farther away from my immediate objective. Fortunately, the Smithean lineage in Hobson is strong enough to make the substition of the market for the nation in the diagrammatic representations of the *Geometry* relatively easy. *(cf* § § 19 and 22)

Semmel's criticism has to do with my use of the concept of hegemony. He maintains that 18th and early 19th century France and 20th century Russia are somewhat speciously excluded from the privileged treatment reserved to 20th century Germany, which I have raised to the same status of hegemonic power as Britain and the US. To begin with, France and Russia have not been excluded from the analysis. They are in fact treated as temporary duopolists of world power that failed to conquer world-hegemony, as opposed to Britain and the US which did succeed. This relative obfuscation of French and Soviet hegemonism is a necessary consequence of my choice to restrict the object of representation to those nation-states that have actually established world-hegemonies.[4] Why then privilege 20th century Germany which, according to my own characterization, achieved only a 'momentary hegemony'? Since I cannot rule out that France and the USSR have achieved in their respective times at least 'momentary hegemony', I must agree with Semmel that that is no good reason for privileging Germany. As I see it now, I did the right thing but gave the wrong justification. What really justifies the preferential treatment granted to Germany is not that it momentarily succeeded in establishing its own hegemony, but rather that it succeeded in permanently destroying the existing hegemonic

[3] Cf G. Arrighi, T. K. Hopkins, I. Wallerstein, 'Rethinking the Concepts of Class and Status Group in a World-System Perspective', *Review*, VI, 3, 1983.

[4] In the Introduction (p. 34) I justify this choice with 'the necessity to keep the puzzle within the limits of my ability to solve it'. On second thought, a more important reason is that a good part of the puzzle would not otherwise have a solution: it is only by introducing the concept of 'hegemonic power', as done at the beginning of chapter II, that a univocal representation of historical time becomes possible: cf pp. 56 and 85n.

order, something that neither France in the early 19th century nor the USSR after World War II succeeded in doing. What really matters, in other words, is the success of what we might call Germany's 'negative hegemony or leadership' throughout the period of rivalry that separates the decline of British hegemony from the establishment of American hegemony. (cf § 14)

I have impinged here on another criticism by Semmel, one that concerns an alleged shortcoming of the maps in representing what they are supposed to represent (or, of my classification procedure): 'Arrighi's chapter describing the "trajectories of United States and German Imperialism", an effort to make them seem a twentieth-century reduplication of earlier British experience, is unfortunately not persuasive. Certainly neither Germany nor the United States re-created Britain's historic path from I_1 to I_4. He succeeds somewhat better in the case of America, but to some degree because of imprecision of language. . . . [It] can readily be argued . . . that America after 1945, like Britain after 1815, entered not the I_2 but the I_3 stage of informal empire, since the United States like Britain in the early nineteenth century, enjoyed an economic preponderance regulated by free market forces. This is certainly Arrighi's decisive differentation between I_2 and I_3, regardless of certain "formal" aspects of American hegemony.'[5]

In answering this criticism the first point I would like to make is that Chapter III does not try at all to make the *trajectories* of United States and German imperialism seem a reduplication of earlier British experience. On the contrary, it tries to show that Germany in her attempt to retread Britain's path was caught in a vicious circle that prevented her from establishing hegemony; and that the United States did establish world-hegemony by

[5] *Op. cit.*, pp. 76–77. I am not quite sure how to handle Semmel's related criticism (omitted in the above quotation) of an alleged confusion on my part between 'empire' and 'expansion' in a context where the former clearly means hierarchy. I see no necessary contradiction between the establishment of a hierarchical world order and expansion. Indeed, all four axes in the diagrams are supposed to represent different forms of expansion of the nation-state, even though only two of them (informal empire and imperialism) are assumed to be stable tendencies in a world dominated by nationalism.

imp: why Volcker & MNG
rule, & administrations 2y
seem to fail

Afterword 167

skipping the phase of nationalist imperialism. What is being
reduplicated in the chapter are not the trajectories but the
theoretical map that defines them. It is precisely this distinction
between historical paths and theoretical map – the theoretical
map on which the paths may be traced – that Fig 11 (p. 90) and
the accompanying discussion attempt to clarify and illustrate.
(cf also p. 59n)

A different question is whether I have correctly located the
American path on the theoretical map, that is to say, whether
between 1945 and 1968 the formal aspects (as I think) or the
informal aspects (as Semmel thinks) were predominant in
American hegemony. I shall not repeat what I have already
stated in the book to justify my position.[6] I shall simply
comment on Semmel's remark that the United States, after 1945,
like Britain after 1815, 'enjoyed an economic preponderance
regulated by free market forces'. While I agree on the parallel
between the economic preponderance of the United States after
1945 and that of Britain after 1815, I strongly disagree on the
characterization, 'regulated by free market forces'.

The disagreement is twofold. In the first place, as I argue
particularly in chapter IV, the main substantive trait of the
postwar American order is not free trade, as it had been for the
British 19th century order, but free enterprise. It is therefore
with reference to the development of a system of transnational
enterprises that the transition from a formal to an informal
world order after 1968 has to be defined. In the second place,
before 1968 the formal aspects of American hegemony in the
crucial military and monetary spheres were absolutely predominant over the informal aspects, that is, a system of
transnational enterprises with some kind of self-regulatory
capacity.[7]

I shall return to this question in section III. For the time being
it remains to deal with the third criticism levelled at the
geometrical metaphor, namely that, introduced as a representation, it is at times treated like an instrument of analysis

[6] I have further explicated my position in 'A Crisis of Hegemony' in S. Amin *et
al.*, *Dynamics of Global Crisis*, New York and London 1982.
[7] See 'A Crisis of Hegemony'.

MNCs didn't want
Viet War

capable of producing conclusions of the order of Cartesian geometry, which it does not and cannot do. I have warned the reader in the Introduction that the topological space constructed in the book remains pre-mathematical in the sense that known theorems do not apply to it (p. 32). I have been very aware of this throughout the book, and I just do not know where I made the geometrical metaphor produce conclusions it could not produce. My critics do not mention any specific instance in which I might have done that. I suspect, however, that what they have in mind are those instances in which I establish points of relative stability and instability for the various tendencies/processes depicted in the diagrams, by 'adding up' the direction of arrows and arcs, either without decoding the terms of the operation or without adducing direct evidence in support of the statements derived from the operation.

Two issues are involved here. The first, at least implicitly, has already been dealt with: the reason why I did not always decode the terms of the operations formed on the diagrams is that my purpose was to construct maps rather than a narrative; and the reason why I did not always substantiate the statements obtained through such 'operations' as I performed is that my main concern was with the historical relevance of explicated premises, not with the validity of hypotheses. The second issue involved is whether the operations performed are themselves legitimate in terms of the meanings assigned to arcs and arrows. I will try to resolve this second issue by showing that the kinds of operations I have been performing make perfect sense once they are translated into ordinary language.

The primitive or basic terms and hypotheses, defined or stated in relation to one another in chapter I, do not in themselves allow any kind of 'operation'. Formally, they are a vocabulary without a syntax; substantively, they define the contradictory forms and tendencies of 'expansionism' in a world dominated by nationalism without giving us any clue as to what they might 'add up to'. It is the definition of hegemonic power in chapter II that gives us such a clue and provides the vocabulary with a syntax. The expansionist policies pursued by the hegemonic state are differentiated from those pursued by other nation-states by designating them with an arc (rather than an arrow along one of the two axes). This attributes to the arcs the 'power' of determining the putative outcome of the contradictory expansionist tendencies of the other nation-states. This 'power' of the arcs is nothing other than the symbolic equivalent of the definition of hegemony. That is to say, a state is defined as hegemonic when it has the power of imposing on the world a given model of interaction/integration of nationalist forces. At the same time, a particular form of hegemony is defined as stable (informal empire and imperialism) or unstable (colonialism and formal empire) according to whether it is or is not sustained by tendencies originating within and between non-hegemonic nation states. (see § § 7–8) Hence, throughout chapters II and III, when 'adding up' the directions of arcs and arrows, I was just using the definition of hegemony in abbreviated notation to specify the outcomes of contradictory expansionist tendencies; or, conversely, I was using basic hypotheses concerning non-hegemonic expansionist tendencies to specify the stabilities of different hegemonic policies.

The kind of operations carried out in chapter IV are somewhat but not altogether different. Quite apart from the use of the geometrical metaphor, chapter IV differs from the previous two because it tries to explicate, not the object of theories of imperialism, but the particular explanation of imperialism given by Hobson, namely, that British territorial expansionism at the turn of the century could be traced to the ensemble of tendencies he refers to as 'finance capitalism'.

Even here, however, my main concern was not to assess the empirical/historical validity of this claim. Such an assessment lay well outside the scope of the essay (as well as outside my competence). My concern was rather to show that the plausibility of Hobson's thesis depends to a very large extent on a precise definition of what he referred to, not only as imperialism, but also as finance capitalism. In order to do this it was necessary to draw a clear distinction between the ensemble of tendencies Hobson was referring to and the economic expansionist tendencies that have figured most prominently in the capitalist world-economy since the Second World War (i.e.

supranational finance capital vs transnational industrial capital). It seemed to me that, at least from the point of view of the coordination of the world division of labour, supranational finance capital and transnational industrial capital are not only distinct concepts but opposites (cf § § 23–24). This new couple of opposites allowed me to add a third dimension to the topological space derived from Hobson, one that I saw as highlighting the difference between the formal and informal phases of the *pax Americana*, on the one hand, and the formal and informal phases of the *pax Britannica* on the other.

The addition of this third dimension undoubtedly complicates the diagrammatic representation. Yet, from the point of view of the operations performed, it merely substitutes arrows designating tendencies characteristic of supranational economic forces for arcs designating tendencies characteristic of hegemonic powers. This substitution follows, as a matter of simple logic, from Hobson's hypothesis that the latter tendencies should be traced causally to the former tendencies. Once this hypothesis is accepted, the 'adding up' of the directions of arrows lying on the plane defined by the coordinates S^--NS-S^+ and N^+-NS-N^- and arrows connecting such a plane to points external to it, as done in figures 13 through 16, is an operation logically equivalent to that of 'adding up' the directions of arcs and arrows discussed above.

We may of course reject Hobson's thesis. As it should be abundantly clear by now, however, this was not my concern. What I wanted to show is simply that, *once thoroughly explicated*, classical theories of imperialism in general and Hobson's version in particular, 1) make more sense than critics and apologists normally accord to them; 2) within the historical limits defined by their premises, they display considerable postdictive and predictive power; and 3) whether plausible or not within their historical domains, they have become totally irrelevant for an understanding of the expansionist phenomena of the post World War II years up through the present.

III

At certain points in the book, remarks can be found to the effect, on the one hand, that it is unlikely that theories of imperialism will regain their classical currency and, on the other, that the entire topological space used in the book will cease to be pertinent with the expected decline in the centrality of the nation-state in world historical developments (cf §24). Since some readers may feel misgivings at these observations, let me clarify their scientific status.

To begin with, in the first three chapters, absolutely nothing is said concerning a possible *future* relevance, as opposed to the seeming present irrelevance of classical theories of imperialism. On the contrary, since the attempt to map the premises of current and classical theories of imperialism had led me to establish a cycle of expansionist tendencies, one might directly infer that sooner or later, in my judgement, the cycle would again run through stage I_4, the imperialism of Hobson's study. And, indeed, in the last section of chapter III I pose the question: 'Is Hobson's concept of imperialism (that is, precisely I_4) of purely historiographical interest, or may it rather gain fresh topicality in the future?' (p. 108).

The answer I give in the negative in chapter IV is based on unsubstantiated hypotheses. As I have repeatedly stated, my aim was the reconstruction of a concept and theory rather than the validation/invalidation of interpretative hypotheses. Bearing this in mind, the reader will understand that what I undertook in chapter IV was only the explication of Hobson's concept of finance capital, for which purpose I used my own notion of multinational capital, a notion formed partly by my drawing on existing hypotheses and characterizations and partly by my filling in the gaps with new hypotheses that served my analytic purpose. Accordingly, while I suggested some illustrations of the contrasting conception, I made no attempt whatsoever to substantiate in any way the claims built into or generated by the construction. It follows that whether theories of imperialism will again become relevant in a more or less distant future remains an historically open question. In the meantime, the maps retain all their usefulness in helping us to assess whether we continue to remain in I_3 (the current phase of informal American hegemony) or are passing through $N-$ into a new imperialist/mercantilist phase proper, I_4, or are moving onto an altogether different plane of hegemonic relations, one no longer defined by – and so undefinable in terms of – the expansionist tendencies of nation-states.

Assuming however that my unsubstantiated hypotheses are not incorrect, but reflect current real trends in the world-economy, what is the essential contemporary pertinence of the book? There is, of course, a permanent historiographical interest in clarifying theoretical issues relating to past expansionist phenomena. But in my opinion the main significance of this work lies in its anticipation, as mentioned at the beginning of this Afterword, of a theory of world-hegemony. For me this was an unintended result of the theoretical reconstruction pursued in the *Geometry*, and it is only in retrospect that I have come to realize that it may prove of more far-reaching interest as such a preface than as a work of critique, its originally intended significance.

That the concept of hegemonic power plays a crucial role in the reconstruction has already been emphasized. Suffice it to say that the reconstruction has implied a re-definition of the various types of 'imperialism' as phases of a cycle of hegemony. Yet, by focussing on theories of imperialism, I was led to qualify with attributes (nationalist, formal, informal, *tout court*), rather than to do away with the term imperialism in designating the phases of hegemony. A far more appropriate designation, I now believe, would have been to define nominally the phases of formal and informal imperialism (I_2 and I_3, respectively) as phases of formal and informal hegemony, and the phases of imperialism *tout court* and of nationalist imperialism (I_4 and I_1 respectively) as phases of latent and open rivalry or struggle for hegemony.[8]

[8] Latent, in the sense that a world-hegemonic power can still be identified, even if its capacity to perform functions of global regulation is jeopardized by challenges of would-be hegemonic powers. Open, in the sense that no world-hegemonic power can be identified, and struggle for hegemony has become the dominant characteristic of the inter-state system.

Redefining the terms in this way is not a purely semantic exercise. Imperialism, in both Hobson's (I_4) and Lenin's (I_1) sense, would come to be conceptualized as forms of rivalry or struggle for world-hegemony, which is something quite different from their conceptualization as forms of capitalist competition, as done in classical theories of imperialism. New questions would be opened up for investigation: in a capitalist world-economy, is the struggle for world-hegemony merely a manifestation of the competitive struggle, as implicitly assumed by theories of imperialism, or is the former a partially autonomous phenomenon capable of determining the context of the competitive struggle itself? To what extent can the power struggle among states, 'vision' and 'leadership' in the inter-state system, military technology and the like be said to organize the patterns of competition and exploitation in the world-economy?

The concepts reconstructed or developed in the *Geometry* could, without difficulty I believe, be recast using the terms of a theory of hegemony that is formed with such questions centrally in mind. In addition, they suggest other hypotheses and questions that such a theory might usefully focus on. They suggest, for example, that each cycle of hegemony is related to a different type of supra/transnationality of capital and that these differences in type may account for differences in the trajectories of world-hegemonies. More specifically, they suggest that the particular form of transnationality of capital associated with American world-hegemony pushes the world system towards forms of global regulation that rely far less than in previous world-hegemonies on the domination of a single *true?* nation-state.

In opening up these kinds of questions, the *Geometry* provides a bridge to move from the now obsolete analytical frameworks built around the expansionist phenomena of the early 20th century to the theoretical problems posed by contemporary expansionist phenomena. I can only hope that others besides myself will find it a useful, albeit awkward, bridge.

November 1982

Bibliography

A. Aguilar, *Pan-Americanism from Monroe to the Present*, New York 1965.

S. Amin, 'Une crise structurelle' in Amin et al., *La crise de l'imperialisme*, Paris 1975.

P. A. Baran and P. M. Sweezy, 'Notes on the Theory of Imperialism' in *Problems of Economics and Planning: Essays in Honor of Michal Kalecki*, Warsaw 1966.

M. Barratt Brown, *After Imperialism*, London 1963.

M. Barratt Brown, *The Economics of Imperialism*, Harmondsworth 1974.

G. Deleuze, 'Par quoi se reconnaît le structuralisme?' in F. Châtelet (ed.) *Histoire de la philosophie*, Vol. 8, *Le XX siècle*, Paris 1973.

M. Dobb, *Political Economy and Capitalism*, London 1940.

M. Dobb, *Studies in the Development of Capitalism*, London 1963.

A. Emmanuel, 'White Settler Colonialism and the Myth of Investment Imperialism', *New Left Review* 73, May–June 1972.

L. Ferrari Bravo, 'Vecchie e nuove questioni nella teoria dell' imperialismo', Introduction to idem. (ed.) *Imperialismo e classe operaia multinazionale*, Milan 1975.

D. K. Fieldhouse, '"Imperialism": An Historiographical Revision', *Econ. Hist. Rev.*, XIV, 2, 1961.

A. G. Frank, *Capitalism and Underdevelopment in Latin America*, New York 1967.

J. Gallagher and R. Robinson, 'The Imperialism of Free Trade', *Econ. Hist. Rev.*, VI, 1, August 1953.

F. Gambino, 'Composizione di classe e investimenti diretti statunitensi all' estero', in Ferrari Bravo (ed.),

Imperialismo e classe operaia multinazionale,

N. Girvan, 'Economic Nationalists vs. Multinational Corporations: Revolutionary or Evolutionary Change?' IDEP, Dakar 1974.

R. F. Harrod, *Money*, London 1969.

K. Hayashi, 'Japan and Germany in the Inter-war Period', in J. W. Morley (ed.), *Dilemmas of Growth in Prewar Japan*, Princeton 1971.

R. Hilferding, *Das Finanzkapital*, Vienna 1923.

C. Hill, *Reformation to Industrial Revolution*, London 1967.

E. J. Hobsbawm, *Industry and Empire*, London 1968.

J. A. Hobson, *Imperialism: A Study*, London 1938.

S. Hymer, 'The Multinational Corporation and the Law of Uneven Development' in J. N. Bhagwati (ed.) *Economics and World Order*, New York 1970.

K. E. Knorr, *British Colonial Theories 1570–1850*, Toronto 1944.

T. S. Kuhn, *The Structure of Scientific Revolutions*, in *International Encyclopaedia of Social Sciences*, Vol. II No. 1, Chicago 1962.

V. I. Lenin, *Imperialism, the Highest Stage of Capitalism*, in *Selected Works* Vol. 1, Moscow 1972.

V. I. Lenin, 'Preface' to N. Bukharin, *Imperialism and World Economy*, London 1925.

V. I. Lenin, 'Address to the Second All-Russian Congress of Communist Organizations of the Peoples of the East', in *Selected Works* Vol. 3, Moscow 1972.

G. Lichtheim, *Imperialism*, Harmondsworth 1974.

H. Magdoff, *The Age of Imperialism*, New York 1969.

W. Markov, *Sistemi coloniali e movimenti di liberazione*, Rome 1961.

K. Marx, 'The Eighteenth Brumaire of Louis Bonaparte', in *Surveys from Exile*, Penguin/NLR 1973.

R. Murray, 'The Internationalization of Capital and the Nation State', *New Left Review* 67, May–June 1971.

F. Neumann, *Behemoth*, London 1942.

J. O'Connor, 'The Economic Meaning of Imperialism', in Fann and Odges (eds.) *Readings in US Imperialism*, Boston 1971.

J. Piaget, *Le structuralisme*, Paris 1968.
K. Polanyi, *The Great Transformation*, Boston 1957.
M. M. Postan, *An Economic History of Western Europe 1945–1964*, London 1967.

J. Schumpeter, *Imperialism – Social Classes*, New York 1955.
F. Schurmann, *The Logic of World Power*, New York 1974.
G. Stedman Jones, 'The History of US Imperialism', in R. Blackburn (ed.) *Ideology in Social Science*, London 1972.
J. Strachey, *The End of Empire*, London 1959.
H. Stretton, *The Political Sciences*, London 1969.
B. Sutcliffe, 'Conclusions', in Owen and Sutcliffe (eds.) *Studies in the Theory of Imperialism*, London 1972.
P. M. Sweezy, *The Theory of Capitalist Development*, London 1946.
P. M. Sweezy, 'The Resurgence of Financial Control: Fact or Fancy?' *Monthly Review*, XXIII, 6, November 1971.

G. Therborn, 'From Petrograd to Saigon', *New Left Review* 48, March–April 1968.

R. W. van Alstyne, *The Rising American Empire: Its Historical Pattern and Evolution*, London 1960.

I. Wallerstein, 'The Rise and Future Demise of the World Capitalist System: Concepts for Comparative Analysis', *Comparative Studies in Society and History*, XVI, 4, September 1974.
I. Wallerstein, *The Modern World System*, New York 1974.
M. Weber, *On the Methodology of the Social Sciences*, New York 1949.
W. A. Williams, *The Contours of American History*.
W. A. Williams, 'The Large Corporation and American Foreign Policy', in D. Horowitz (ed.) *Corporations and the Cold War*, New York 1969.
C. Wilson, *Mercantilism*, London 1958.

Index

mes <u>remember</u>: new Soviet threat
as <u>ritual</u>, to corral allies &
mask U.S. dominance (Kaldor)

Reaganism: – restoration, Indian Summer
- another Hoves
- another rollback
- another Asia-first
- but, masks a new
  internat'lism of MNCs,
  who organize Asia
- china wavering is key
  to this in Reagan yrs.
- Trilateralism won:
  US econ, hegemony